TulipTree
review

SPRING/SUMMER 2020
issue #8

Wild Women

TULIPTREE
PUBLISHING, LLC

Contents

Eve: I Did It on Purpose

Melina Vanchieri

We were sheep—
two lambs of God—
frolicking in the Garden,
with all the blissful ignorance
of dumb animals.

"Would you rather live in a gilded cage,
plump on birdseed like a glossy-feathered canary?
Or fly free?" asked the Angel.

He had a point.

We were dust,
innocent dust,
made like dolls to praise the Almighty.
Adam was content.
I was confined.

The lush Garden with its trees and that high wall loomed over me,
verdant shade blocking the sun from my eyes.
Paradise with all the food we would ever need,
but I wasn't hungry for fruit.

The sun toasted my naked back as I climbed,
slick mossy rocks biting my knees as I slipped.
Soft and uncalloused, my hands betrayed me.
I fell.

Adam was curious,
he had never seen a bruise.
The Creator narrowed his eyes.
I could hear the wall growing higher.

I paced, a trapped animal.
The eyes of the Angel were on me.
"Help," I said.

In whispers I learned of another.
A disobedient voice echoing in the trees.
A shallow tunnel, wide enough for one woman,
now stopped with rocks and mud.

I dug, nails broken and packed with dirt.
I heard a Voice on high,
and felt a rumble as the wall grew deeper.

I was throwing apples in silent anger.
Adam watched them burst against the wall.
"Why?" he asked.

Why?

Why a tiny garden in a world unexplored?
Why a wall so high to block it out?
Why a captive audience,
free to worship, but never free?

He sighed and hefted an apple.
It splattered next to mine.
The Angel smiled.

I bought our freedom with a sharp tongue,
facing rumbles of anger like the cracking of a storm cloud.
Unfazed, I argued.
Disrespect buying pain while giving birth,
and a new feature in that wall.

It was a door.

The Angel laughed as we left,
his parting gift a pocket full of apples
in a coat made of fig leaves.

The sun was blinding to our shaded eyes.
The ground harsh,
cutting at feet usually cushioned with grass.
In the distance
lightning as thick as a river struck inside the Garden.

The Angel screamed as he fell.
While we flew free.

That Kiss

Sue Staats

EVERYTHING ABOUT BEVERLY WAS RICH AND EXTRAVAGANT—HER SIZE, HER gestures, the way her home was, at all seasons, filled with luscious aromas—yeast and spices, apples, savory roasts, tangy sauces. Her gardens were never dormant—whatever the time of year they burst with color, especially now, in April, with everything in bloom and the bees fighting each other to feast at the biggest, most extravagant flowers. And how, amid all this lushness, could she have just given her husband George such a sad, anemic little peck of a kiss?

She was astonished—no, *ashamed*—that it came from her mouth, this bland, flaccid thing, this kiss without appetite, this miserable *excuse* for a kiss.

Even worse, it was the same kiss she gave him every day as he left for work. She brushed a speck from the shoulder of his suit with the wisp of a wish that things could be different.

And maybe it was the slight push of that wish, or maybe it was the hint of cinnamon from his breakfast toast still on her mouth, or the soft breeze lifting the delicate hairs on the back of her hand, or maybe it was the face turned toward hers, his face, that she loved in spite of the years and the sags and lines and extra flesh—whatever it was, in that moment, without thinking, she slid her hand up the breast of his suit coat and kissed him again, really kissed him this time, deeply and richly, with plenty of juicy tongue and oh, wonderful, he didn't hesitate, he returned the kiss and wrapped his arms around her, not as far as he used to when they first kissed like this, when such kisses would lead to his being late for work, but enough.

They parted, stunned. She thought of the laundry, and the dishes in the sink, and that she should go back into the house, but the early morning sun was washing them in the loveliest, most lucid light, and she pulled him back to her for another kiss, even less chaste than the first. The neighbors be damned.

George staggered back. Locked in their embrace, she stumbled after. He managed to grab the railing, so they didn't tumble into the budding hydrangea. They separated, breathing heavily. Neither of them was used to so much exercise, or such daring, unexpected behavior, and on their front porch, for all to see. These days, George didn't usually like surprises. Beverly hoped today was different.

But George disengaged himself and frowned slightly. Beverly couldn't help it—she sighed with disappointment.

"Really, Beverly," George said. He wiped his mouth. "The neighbors."

He straightened his tie, turned, and stepped away from her, down their flagstone front walk. His suit jacket flapped open. Oh dear, his pants were too tight again. They couldn't be let out any more; she'd have to think of a way to suggest a new suit in a larger size without embarrassing him.

As he opened the car door he turned and waved to her. "Tonight, then," he called. She waved back with a small formal gesture, like the queen, who must occasionally feel the same discontent she was feeling, in spite of all her wealth and jewels and a prince for a husband.

But, that kiss. She licked her lips. She tasted toothpaste, the numbness of peppermint and then, masked but definitely there, a savory, complex, slightly sulfurous yet not unpleasant tang that she recognized as the aftertaste of his breakfast eggs, lingering on the tip of her tongue. The toothpaste was pleasant, but it didn't make her think intriguing twisty thoughts in the same way the hint of eggs was doing.

And the day! What a day! In the weeping cherry next to the front porch, the usually shy little gray bushtits tumbled and sang, so careless with lust they didn't notice how close they came to her. She lifted her face and closed her eyes. All winter she'd felt suffocated, like an insect in a jar with the lid screwed down tight. But this morning, all of that seemed swept away by kisses and by the jumble of odors, too tangled to identify, riding the early April breeze. She'd heard robins whistle before dawn, pollen coated the car windshields, and, most intriguing of all, there'd been an invasion of skunks, filling the night air with their musky, metallic, intriguing scent. Every day, someone complained about their dog being sprayed. Recipes for getting rid of the stink were the new currency of Olive Street.

"You two kids. I swear." From across the street her friend Janet called, wagging a finger. "Naughty," she said.

Beverly laughed and rolled her eyes.

"Come over for coffee," Janet said, then told her she'd seen a skunk trotting up her driveway not an hour before, just at dawn.

"My driveway?" Beverly said, and was about to cross the street but stopped when she heard the low purr of a car's engine and saw their neighbor Patrick backing out of his driveway. He eased his sleek black Porsche between them, stopped, said something to Janet, and glanced at Beverly. Janet's finger trailed a faint path in the car's shine, and Beverly noticed that her usually ponytailed hair fell loose down her back. A widow, Janet had moved to Olive Street nearly a year ago, just after her husband died. They watched as Patrick turned the corner and drove past the park, on his way downtown.

"Coffee?" Janet said again across the now-empty street. She wrapped her silk bathrobe tighter, pinched the collar with her long freckled fingers. It was a kimono splashed with watercolor roses, different from the frayed green one she usually wore.

For weeks, Beverly had been hearing shrieks she assumed were neighborhood cats, but last night she'd flung the bedroom window open to let in the soft spring air and she'd heard the sound again but closer, and realized it was coming from Patrick's house, from his bedroom, just a few feet away across the narrow driveway. The yowls bloomed and subsided and ricocheted off the stucco surface and were so loud and long and intentional that Beverly thought no, it can't be cats. And then someone laughed and a woman's voice said *really* and laughed some more and suddenly she knew it was Janet.

"I heard you and Patrick last night," Beverly said and immediately clamped her hand over her mouth. "His window was open."

The words came out muffled but they shouldn't have come out at all. What was going on? Since the skunks appeared, all her careful boundaries seemed to be redrawing themselves, maybe even disappearing entirely.

Janet pursed her lips. "Really?" she said, with the same intonation Beverly had heard, then she laughed and Beverly felt a surge of energy, like she was entering rooms in an enormous house filled with secrets. Sunlight fired across the park, through the tender new leaves, lighting the red gold of Janet's hair. Janet scanned the street for listeners.

"I don't know what I'm doing, you know," she whispered. "But it's pretty amazing." She laughed again. "We'll close the window."

No, no, don't! Beverly wanted to say. It was such a private pleasure, to be awake at night with all that fervid activity not fifteen feet away and George, dear George, chuffing in his sleep beside her, the rolls on his neck piled up like the blubber on a walrus. Hearing Janet and Patrick was as close to actual sex as she'd had in years. She used to love it. *They* used to love it.

Over coffee in her kitchen Janet chatted, more animated than Beverly had ever seen her, about the unexpected new events in her life. "I feel like a teenager," she said. Beverly told her she looked wonderful, which she did, thinking that the sheen and glow of Janet's skin must be what the fashion magazines meant by the word *dewy*. Beverly wondered what *her* skin looked like.

"All that exercise is agreeing with you," she said. They both giggled.

Later, as she was walking up her driveway toward the back gate, Beverly noticed that the screened cover to the crawl space beneath the house was open. She latched it back up. Paperwhite narcissus in tight bud massed in a tangle of green against the pale stucco. A little more sun and they'll be open, she thought, and passed through her back gate into a shower of orange blossoms.

THAT NIGHT, AS GEORGE slept, Beverly opened the bedroom windows wide again and drowsed into the most delicious dream, in which she was young and slender and slipping between the trees of an orchard with a man, maybe George, maybe not George. The man touched her arm; she could see the curve of his upper lip and smell his breath. It was heavy with the familiar scent of orange and something else—what was it? Hints of something oily, something acrid, and there was thumping. She jerked awake. The clock blinked green: two-thirty.

George stood next to the bed. In the pellucid light, his belly loomed white over boxer shorts. "Hear that? The cat's brought a mouse in." Beverly heard sharp trills and twitters, coming from somewhere close, maybe the next room. "Muffin!" he shouted, clapping his hands and stamping his feet.

The floor shuddered under his weight and a thunderclap of skunk stench burst from beneath the floorboards and shot into the room, blooming so strong and metallic Beverly could taste it.

"It's not inside," she said, swoony with the smell. "It's outside. I mean, under. Under the house."

George bent over, coughing and gagging. "What the hell are they doing?"

"Mating, George. Mating. Like everything else." She sat up. Oh, the bushtits caught up in their lust, the pollen everywhere, Janet's rosy cheeks. "For God's sake, George, they're having sex. It's spring." Her breasts swung under her cotton nightgown. "Everyone's doing it." She threw her arms wide. "Sex, sex, sex!" she shouted. "It's everywhere! We even kissed!"

George froze. Silence and a skunky cloud wrapped them.

"Beverly, what the hell is the matter with you?" He grabbed his pillow. "I'm sleeping in the guest room. You coming?"

"No." She tilted her head in what she hoped was a saucy look. "I like it."

"Like what?"

"The smell."

"I swear to God, Beverly . . ." His voice trailed off as he closed the door, then opened it again. "I'm calling an exterminator in the morning." His feet thudded down the hall.

Beverly lay back and spread her legs into the warm space he'd left behind. The fine foggy essence of skunk curled into her lungs and snaked deliciously through her bronchi. She was sliding back down into sleep when the moans from next door began, crescendoed, then subsided. She heard giggles, a sudden shriek of laughter, whispers. Patrick and Janet, again!

Their window slammed shut.

Beverly had never seen Patrick's bedroom, but she imagined it a perfect cave for seduction: the walls a deep satiny brown, tiny track lighting, a king-sized bed with silky, copper-colored sheets, the smells of musk and Janet's lily-of-the-valley perfume and the sweet punk of half-eaten cartons of takeout Chinese and strewn items of clothing. And oh dammit *Janet* was languid in those sheets, and *her* body was tangled with Patrick's and Beverly was just . . . tangled.

All around her the night shuffled and stirred. Beverly's nightgown had scrunched up between her thighs and she flapped the fabric loose. Deep in her belly she felt a fluttering she hadn't felt in a long time. Wisps of skunk still drifted, random sparks from a dying campfire.

Oh, George. Decades ago, *their* howling must have entertained the couple who used to live in Patrick's house. But then he'd had a few embarrassing failures, and she'd gotten—well—dryer, then they'd both put on some weight and all of those years of added pounds and decreasing desire just piled on and wore her out, wore them out, and now sex with George seemed impossible. Beverly couldn't remember when they'd last tried.

She missed him.

Soft squeaks trilled from beneath the house, sounding content, as if the skunks were nuzzling each other. Beverly sighed and reached for her own familiar wetness. After a minute or two she stopped. *What's the worst that can happen?* she thought. *He'll say no. Nobody will die. I can still come back to this. Come on, Beverly. What would Janet do?*

Janet would be howling at the moon by now, she thought. Rising and padding barefoot across the hall, she paused at the doorway to the guest room and pulled her nightgown over her head, tossing it onto the floor.

She slid in beside George. The sheets were cool on her side of the bed, and she spooned into his back, curved her arm across his body. He gave a little grunt of surprise. "You're naked."

She wiggled against him. "I am."

"You're a little skunky," he said.

"Pepé le Pew would find me irresistible," she said, speaking into the softness of his back. He smelled clean, like sun-dried sheets. He always did. He was silent and she considered withdrawing her arm, but he took her hand, breathed in its scent, and pressed the palm to his lips.

"Ah, oui, oui," he said. "Ze smell of *amour.*"

Beverly giggled, embarrassed. "Not my fault," she said. "I heard Patrick having sex."

"You *heard* him?"

"You know how sounds carry in the driveway. Guess with who?"

"With *whom.*"

"Oh, *who, whom,* who cares, Professor le Pew. It was Janet."

"Across-the-street Janet?"

"Yes." She tilted her pelvis against the small of his back. "Janet. Everyone's doing it, George." She disengaged her fingers and slid her hand over his belly. "The birds, the bees, the neighbors. Us."

George stopped her hand, rolled onto his back, and glanced at her, then stared at the ceiling, his eyes reflective as soap bubbles in the pale light. Beverly rose up on one elbow and he turned back to her with a look she'd always interpreted as disapproval but she could see now might be fear.

"Please," she said, tracing slow circles on his skin. "Let's just try."

"No," he said. His arms tensed and his belly felt hard as a basketball.

"It's scary for me too," she said. "George, honey."

"It won't work." He'd gripped her hand again, stopping her. She shook her fingers free and forced them between his thighs and found his penis, curled like a baby.

"Let's just breathe," she said. "See what happens."

"Nothing will happen," he said, his voice tight.

"Just try it. Ten breaths. Just ten."

After the fifth breath she took him in her hand, gently. After the tenth breath his belly softened. "This is nice, just like this," she said.

She had not been expecting anything to happen. But something was. And for a minute, she thought he wasn't aware of it. But he was. "Holy shit," he whispered, and then his body arched upward. Beverly scissored her legs over him and he cupped her buttocks, guiding him into her. They both let out a soft, surprised cry and Beverly felt a rush of pleasure, sweet and sour, bitter and sweet, a mosaic interlaced with the smell of skunk, which was neither bitter nor sweet but something else, something more—the pinch of espresso in chocolate, adding depth and richness, the drop of lime juice stirred into a silky sauce, intensifying its perfection.

Beverly dug her fingers into his flesh, rocking, breathing in their combined smell: a little lemony, a little funky. He finished and she lay on him for a bit. They both sighed. When she lay back beside him he fell asleep immediately.

She thought she'd be wakeful but the next thing she knew the morning sun was reddening her eyelids, waking her. When she stepped onto her front porch for the newspaper Janet was running across the street carrying her shoes. She waved to Beverly and sashayed into her house with a little flip of her hips as she closed the door. Beverly laughed and walked barefoot across the wet lawn, then up the path at the side of the house. The door to the crawl space was open again.

Sweeping aside a few trailing branches of bridal veil bush she knelt next to the opening, scooped up a handful of soil, and inhaled the loamy, skunky smell. It wasn't enough. She wanted more, more. She lowered her face and sniffed along the wood framing and the odor was deeper, tangier. In the darkness under the house, in the space directly beneath their bedroom, two pairs of small, shining eyes fixed on hers.

"Hi, you two," she said. She knelt and hunkered down, making herself smaller, cupping her hands against the house, shading her eyes so she could see better: two black noses, a white stripe bisecting each face, huddled in the cool dirt. What did they think of the thudding feet, the voices above? Did they smell her? Did they smell George? For a moment she wished herself next to them, maybe even as dramatically beautiful, black and white with a queenly brush of a tail.

A horn honked several streets away. How outrageous she must look, outside in her nightgown, ass in the air, sniffing at the dirt, looking for all the world as if she was trying to squeeze herself under her own house. Anyone could see her.

She rocked back on her knees. The morning was rich with the green scent of new leaves, the metallic smell of the asphalt street, the resin-y odor of wet cedar fence, the smell of her own yeasty body rising from the heat of her belly. Next to her, the paper-white narcissus had opened, freeing their heavy fragrance. Beverly picked one of the blooms, then plucked two, then three, then bunches. The stems oozed sap; her hands and arms were smeared with it.

Pipes gurgled inside the house. George was up.

She carried the flowers around to the kitchen door. George stood at the stove, laying strips of bacon in the skillet. His belly strained the limits of her frilly apron. His scalp shone through sparse hairs. At the sound of her opening the door he turned his head toward her and his whole face lit with a smile, and his eyes gleamed in a way she hadn't seen in years. A forgotten strip of bacon dangled from his fingers.

"Beautiful," he breathed, seeing her.

Beverly lifted her chin, cradled the blooms, and stood tall in the doorway. She had never been beautiful, but now it was as if her skin had cracked open and a newer, more lustrous version of herself had stepped out and was standing barefoot in her kitchen, dizzy with scent.

"They're under the house, George." She stepped across the threshold.

"They can stay," he said, without a whisper of argument.

A Well-Cut Coat and Bright Smile

Patricia Schultheis

THE LAST EVENING OF AUGUST 1939, AND OLGA KADYKOWSKA AND HER mother are about to have dinner. Before she sits down, Olga's mother flaps her plump little hands at the radio, her habitual gesture of annoyance: too much . . . too much. Germans massing at Poland's border. France and England, allies in name only. Too much. She shuts the radio off. Better to have a nice, quiet meal.

There's even bread—a miracle—hoarding has begun. Olga and her mother eat, synchronized in mind and body, no need for words. Meal done, the two women wash and dry the china, put it away in the burled walnut cabinet under the window. Then Olga's mother turns off the chandelier.

"The E or the F?" Olga asks.

"The E, I think."

Olga winds up the Victrola, puts on Chopin's Concerto in E Minor, Op. 11.

Her mother disappears into the kitchen, returns with a small box of chocolates. A brilliant, beautiful chemistry professor, her smile can work magic, can make bread and chocolate appear out of nowhere. She sits down, opens the box.

Olga eats one with a coconut center, settles back, becomes a tuning fork thrumming with each note. And with wonder—a hundred years before, a young genius wrote a concerto that's been captured on a spinning disk to be freed by a needle to be enjoyed by two women whose spirits survive on harvests of small joys—the improbability of music and chocolates on the brink of war.

From her earliest age, both her parents cultivated in Olga the art of husbanding life's little gifts. But then the coup of 1926 came and her father disappeared, Olga ten at the time. And her mother married a mathematician who didn't understand small joys or anything else about the dynamic between Olga and her mother. He left, leaving nothing of himself except his last name attached to Olga's mother.

The final note fades and she nods toward the remaining chocolates. "Take them, Olga, for the people at work."

"What about the people you work with, Mama?"

"Oh, they . . ." she gives a quick dismissive smile, meaning that unlike the people in the ministry where Olga works, the members of the university chemistry department have more serious concerns than chocolate. Olga puts on her hat, gathers her handbag and the chocolates. Then, her mother does something she's never done before: she rides the elevator down with Olga, follows her through the elegant lobby and onto the building's broad steps.

"Remember, Olga. A well-cut coat and a bright smile can get a woman through a long, cold season." Their aphorism, their joke—her mother having said it two years earlier when Olga got her current position at the ministry and to celebrate her mother gave her a gray wool coat interlined with more wool. And trimmed with astrakhan cuffs. No matter how long the Warsaw winter, whenever she puts it on, Olga feels elegant.

"And now, Mama, I have chocolates too!" She waggles the box.

Her mother gently lifts out the crucifix on a gold chain from beneath Olga's collar.

"Mama?"

"What?"

"Whatever happens, you know—"

Her mother raises her palms to the stars. "What could possibly happen on such a night?"

Just like her mother, Olga thinks, always able to lighten a dark horizon with a twist of irony. Like a few drops of vermouth in a shot of vodka.

Olga's own apartment is on the other side of the park, where, especially on summer nights, young parents push prams and old couples sit side by side on benches. But tonight the park is empty except for a single figure, a gangly boy darting through the shrubs encircling the lake. He reminds Olga of the oldest son of her boss, Mr. Tomkalski. Every Sunday at mass, she sees the boy with his family, but what's he doing here? . . . and is it really him? The figure disappears.

When she reaches her apartment, Olga wonders if she should check on her widowed neighbor, Mrs. Tsarchuk, but then she'd have to offer the old woman the chocolates and she wants them for the people at work. Inside, she bathes at her kitchen sink, doubling over to wash her hair—her looks are a crude copy of her mother's, but she does have her mother's subtle fashion flair and luxuriant hair. She drapes a towel over her shoulders and fans out her hair over it. A drink of that vodka under her sink would be nice. But she focuses on other small joys: the cooling dampness of her hair, her crucifix's golden glow, the watermarked cover of the book by her bed, a German vocabulary that had belonged to her father from the days when he studied in Heidelberg.

She'd been how old—five? six?—when she would sit on his lap and watch his mustache while he intoned, "Die grau kat und der schwarze hund." Oh, the wonderful game he had made of feeding her silly German phrases. Even in high school, where she studied Latin and French, she still managed to retain some German.

"I might let Mr. Tomkalski take the vocabulary book when he visits his brother in Munich," she had told her mother that spring as they were walking to a concert.

Her mother froze. "Olga, no! Maybe it's best not to mention those books to anyone."

"Why would anyone care about some old vocabulary book?"

Her mother's voice had crackled with exasperation. "You're the one who should care. Maybe this mess with Germany will blow over. But if it doesn't, you should have sense enough to realize that knowing a little German can prove valuable." Olga felt like she had when she was fifteen and her mother berated her for hanging out with that slattern Klara Kushka.

What she never tells her mother is that she studies her father's old books for the marginalia he wrote. Tonight, the last night of August 1939, Olga opens the vocabulary to the R's. Beside "regret," she reads, "Anyone who says he has no regrets is either a fool or a liar." Then Olga turns off her light. It is 10:30. Six hours and fifteen minutes of peace remain.

PLANES SO CLOSE THEIR pilots could wink at her through her window rattle Olga awake. She turns on the radio: Chopin's Polonaise in A Flat, what else would they play? Then, an announcement: "The Polish Army, one million strong, is rushing to the front and will defeat . . ." What else would they say? Olga tries calling her mother, but the lines are jammed. She decides to go to work. What else should she do? She does up her hair, checks herself in the mirror, and flips the gold crucifix out of her collar. She's almost out the door when she remembers the chocolates.

The streets are chaos, people running everywhere, especially into the park. At the corner, she sees all the bakery's shelves are empty, a window smashed. The baker is sweeping up the glass. Suddenly a cheer arises from the park. The baker and Olga watch a tree wobble back and forth, then topple. She turns toward him. "What . . . ?"

The baker leans on his broom. "Barricades."

At the ministry, the main office is empty except for her boss. A short man, Mr. Tomkalski is standing unsteadily on a wheeled chair and rifling through folders in a filing cabinet's top drawer. He's tossing out papers, letting them lie wherever they land. Thorough but kind, Mr. Tomkalski is the best boss Olga's ever had, but today he barks without looking at her, "Pick those up. Take them downstairs to the basement. Crazy Old Pozwit has managed to get the furnace going." Olga puts the chocolates down, tries arranging the papers into piles, but her arms can only hold so many. She finds a box in the outer office. Throughout that day her box will become her most valued possession. Every time she hands over a boxful of papers, she will give Old Pozwit a slight, regretful smile—all the ministry's fastidious assessing, compiling, collecting, distributing, all of it going up in flames. And Old Pozwit, a drunken Vulcan tottering before the maw of his furnace, will twist his toothless mouth into a quick commiserative grin.

Late that afternoon, the whole building inhales a deep breath, then resettles itself into a subtle misalignment. Olga's in the elevator. She pushes button after button, but the door will not open. She sits on the floor and screams for help. No one comes. So, she presses her palms against the door and pushes it to the side. Miraculously, it opens, but the floor—she doesn't know which one—is above her waist. She can hoist herself up only by raising a leg, but her dress is too tight. She takes it off and her high heeled shoes too, tosses them out of the elevator, then manages to lever herself out after them. She feels filthy.

She's putting on her shoes when the building sways again. When she gets to the office Mr. Tomkalski is gone, and the box of chocolates is nearly empty. She takes it and leaves. Across the park, in the direction of her mother's apartment, smoke is rising. When she gets home, she tries calling her, but the lines still are jammed.

She's about to walk across the park, when someone knocks on the door. Mrs. Tsarchuk. The old woman stands in the hallway, crying. Olga sits her down by the radio, where the old woman sways back and forth, repeating a single word, "Jósef . . . Jósef," the name of her grandson with the club foot—Olga has seen him coming and going from the old woman's flat. She offers the old woman the remaining chocolates and makes tea. She's about to cook her an egg when the old woman suddenly takes Olga's arm and leads her across the hall to her own apartment, where she cooks two sausages and pours two shots of vodka. Together, they listen to the radio broadcast the news of Poland's inevitable, swift victory.

The next day Olga goes to work, hoping the phones there are working. They're not. As far as she can tell the only people in the ministry are herself and Old Pozwit. When she brings down the last of the papers, he smells of something worse than his usual booze and sweat. He smells like the sewer. Olga leaves the ministry and sees smoke across the park. She starts to her mother's but only gets as far as the lake where a citizen's brigade has formed to douse fires.

There's her mother, her small, plump hands handing one sloshing bucket after another to none other than Klara Kushka. Olga wedges herself between them. "Mama, I was so worried. I saw all the smoke . . . I thought your apartment—"

"It's fine . . . a window broken . . . that's all."

Within five minutes, Olga's arms are ready to fall off; within ten, her back to break. Darkness comes, but the buckets come faster. Her dress and shoes become soaked. Elsewhere more trees are being felled. No cheers now, she notices. Just a crack, a crash, a void. Klara gives her a smile that Olga's too tired to return.

A tall man in a leather jacket walks down the line. "You can stop now. We've got things under control. Time to get home." Olga sees him smile, not at Klara and not at her. But at her mother.

Olga turns to her. "Mama?"

Her mother glances at the man, then puts her hand on Olga's cheek. "Go home, Olga. You look exhausted. Get to bed. We'll get through this, you'll see."

Klara Kushka holds out a pack of cigarettes. "Want one, Olga?"

Olga smiles. "No . . . no."

Klara extends her arm and cocks her head. "Sure? Not even for old time's sake?"

"That's all right, Klara. They're all yours."

The next day is Saturday and Olga cleans her apartment, presses her clothes for the coming week, and studies her father's books.

Later, there seems to be a break in the bombing, so she decides to risk going to confession. On the stairs, she passes Mrs. Tsarchuk's grandson lumbering up.

"Thank you for the chocolates you gave my grandmother, Miss Kadykowska."

"They were nothing."

At church, long lines of penitents wait. Olga kneels outside the confessional of Father Matusik, the old priest who knows that she cheated on her final math exam, that she and Klara had wine when they smoked by the lake, and that she's had a brief love affair. Now she'll kneel to eternity if it means a chance to confess her deepest sin: her soul's despair at God's absence.

The next morning, at mass, she concentrates on the beauty of the sunlight through the stained glass windows—any small joy will do. Across the aisle, Mr. Tomkalski kneels with his family. But not with his oldest boy.

On Monday, Mr. Tomkalski returns to the ministry and has Olga type up brief memos on the latest tax rolls and a proposed new bridge, but they both know these things belong to another life.

The siege continues, and when the water works are destroyed, Olga immediately thinks of Pozwit: the old man is a mechanical genius—if any place will have water, the ministry will. She takes out her vodka and carefully decants a few ounces into a bottle small enough to fit into her handbag. She finds the old man in the ministry's basement and, smiling, takes out her vodka. "Water. Do you have any?"

He reaches for her vodka, but Olga retracts her hand, playfully, but still out of Pozwit's reach. The old man grins. "Come with me." He takes her deeper into the basement. Below a jury-rigged maze of pipes and hoses a faucet drips into a bucket. "How many bottles?" he asks.

"Five."

He eyes her own small bottle. "Four."

Olga smiles. "Four then."

She carries them across the park to her mother's. The elevators aren't working so she carries her precious water up four flights. When she knocks, no one answers, so she uses the key her mother hides beneath a loose tile. Inside, the shattered glass from the window overlooking the park lies like transparent shrapnel over the burled walnut cabinet.

The whole apartment reeks with absence. Olga senses her mother isn't merely out; she's away. Away as her mind had been years ago when Olga would find her sitting at the kitchen table and correcting chemistry papers late into the night. Away in a realm completely alien to Olga.

But then Olga thinks of the basement—half of Warsaw is either going down into or climbing out of basements. She goes down. And there's her mother with the tall man in the leather jacket. Together, they're studying a large map of Warsaw. "Olga!" her mother says.

"I brought you water, Mama. I thought you might need water."

"Oh, water, yes, well, that's good." Her mother glances at the man, then gently takes Olga's elbow and turns her away from the map. "Water . . . however did you get it?" Keeping her grip on Olga's elbow, she leads her to the stairwell. "Listen, Olga, those German books, maybe it would be best if you hid them. When you're not studying them, hide them away. And pay attention to the grammar. Not just the vocabulary."

Olga has an inkling why. "If I found out something, Mama, what would I do with it?"

"Don't worry about that now. Who knows, maybe Poland will win."

The siege continues for two more weeks. The morning after the surrender a German officer sits at Mr. Tomkalski's desk. Olga wonders if she should disregard her mother's warning about not letting anyone know she knows a little German—how else is she going to work with him? But to her relief, Colonel Lichel speaks passable Polish. He tells her how he likes his tea and that most of his letters she'll have to type in duplicate, although some will require triplicate. "Will that be a problem?"

"No, Colonel."

"Good."

She makes certain to wear her crucifix out of her collar. In the first weeks, the colonel's correspondence focuses on two things: the red banners that hang everywhere. Are there enough and properly hung? And two: Warsaw's various districts. How many people live in each? What are their ethnicities? On the phone he speaks German, and Olga tries to train herself to type and listen, but she's hopeless at it. Maybe whatever Colonel Lichel is responsible for isn't important. Maybe she can just make his tea and type until the war ends.

And then, late in October, Colonel Lichel has Olga type a memo about Polish "intelligentsia." He has a list of them, and Olga spots her former stepfather's last name. Only the name before it is her mother's.

"Is something wrong, Miss Kadykowska?"

"No, Colonel. The ribbon was a little jammed, that's all."

That evening, she runs home, gets her winter coat, and dashes through the park. There is a curfew, and the cost for violation is death. But she has to get to her mother. Has to give her her own warm coat. In it, her mother will look like the person Olga has always known: a woman in charge of her own fate.

As soon as her mother opens the door, her expression tells Olga that she already knows why Olga has come. Olga thrusts the coat at her. "Take it, Mama. It's warmer than yours, and you'll look good in it. You'll look like you're just going on a trip somewhere."

Her mother pulls her inside. The window has been boarded up, and a single candle burns near the couch where they listened to Chopin. "No one just goes on a trip anymore, Olga."

"You have to leave, Mama. They have a list."

Her mother presses her finger to Olga's lips. "And how would that look for you, Olga? You working for a senior German administrator, and your mother suddenly nowhere to be found?"

"But the list has *your* name. Not mine."

"They'll still make the connection. The one thing we know for certain about them is that they're not fools."

"Then let's leave together. You and me. Right now."

"And go where? East? West?"

"I don't know . . . I don't know . . ."

Her mother puts her hand on Olga's cheek. "Oh, Olga. You're the best thing that ever happened to me. But you have to go home now. The curfew." Over her mother's shoulder Olga sees someone step out of the bedroom. The tall man.

Her mother walks her out of the flat and into the stairwell. She whispers, "Remember what they say and their memos, Olga. It may prove useful. No matter how insignificant it may seem."

"Mama, I don't know if I can do—"

"Nobody does. All over Poland, people are doing what they don't know they can."

Her mother's still there at Christmas. Olga brings her a loaf of bread and half a chicken breast. The tall man is there too. He produces a bottle of wine. And potatoes! Somehow her mother manages to look both haggard and happy.

When Olga puts on her coat to go home, her mother's hug is so fierce it almost enfolds Olga into herself, as if she's trying to keep Olga in the safest place she'll ever know: her own body.

The clasp of her mother's arms that Christmas impresses itself into Olga's bones.

ON THE SECOND FRIDAY of January, Olga is walking home when someone hooks their arm through hers. Klara Kushka. She smiles and leans in. "So, Olga, tomorrow, you'll go to confession I suppose. You always go to Father Matusik, don't you?"

"How did you know?"

"That's not important. Just tell him whatever you've come across. Whatever you read and hear."

They turn a corner, and two German soldiers saunter toward them. Klara leans in closer. "For God's sake, Olga, smile."

So, Olga does. She even manages to chatter about maybe getting the lining of her coat repaired. As soon as they've passed the Germans, Klara whispers, "Tomorrow, confession, Olga. Remember," and darts into the bakery.

In the confessional, Olga kneels. "A solution," she says. "Whenever he talks to his superiors, he mentions some sort of final solution." When she leaves, Mr. Tomkalski's oldest boy is kneeling outside. Week after week, spring, summer, fall, the boy's there.

January a year later, Olga again kneels in the confessional. "They're amassing barbed wire. Miles of it."

Behind the screen, Father Matusik asks, "What for?"

"I don't know. The coils aren't very large, maybe sixty centimeters."

"Anything else?"

"He wants to put it on top of something, but I don't know what."

Early in March she tells the priest, "He and another officer, Colonel Kessel, they argue about the map of Warsaw. They draw lines, then redraw them. I don't know why."

"For your penance, say three Our Fathers."

Later that month: "They're going to build a wall. The barbed wire is for on top."

On April 1, the construction of the ghetto begins.

When the wall is built, non-Jews are expelled from its area, and a mother and her little girl come to live with Mrs. Tsarchuk. They bring two chickens. The old widow's lame grandson builds a pen in the kitchen. The hens must have met a rooster because they lay eggs holding chicks. Olga tells the old widow she'll ask Pozwit if he'll incubate them by the ministry's furnace. He says he will, if he can keep two chicks for himself. When they hatch, the brood totals nine.

Olga is carrying the remaining seven home when someone's arm encircles her waist. Klara Kushka. She looks five years older than she had earlier. "So, Olga, what do you have there?" But the peeping box gives its contents away. "Give me one." The two women duck into an alley, and Olga watches Klara stash a chick beneath her sweater. "I hope it doesn't peck my tit off. And Olga?"

"What?"

"See if you can find out anything about coal."

"That's another department."

Mrs. Tsarchuk gives Olga a chick for herself. She knows she should raise and kill it, but the chicken becomes a pet. Olga names her Joy. In the evening, Joy sits on her lap while Olga studies German. Whenever she comes across one of her father's comments she traces its letters with her fingertip, as if the letters were the lifeline of her father's living palm. Beside "Semite" he has written, "We are all children of Abraham."

In the confessional, she commits the sin of omission, leaving out some of what she knows . . . what if the Germans connect the feeble acts of sabotage that the Resistance is mounting to her? In addition to her assigned penance, she prays for a speedy, painless death.

The next winter, after work she's putting her key into her lock, when Mrs. Tsarchuk's door opens. "Have you heard?" Inside the old woman's apartment, her grandson has rigged up a radio, a capital offense, but they all listen: The Americans have declared war on Japan. And Germany.

"It won't be long now," says the woman who brought the chickens.

But it is long. Very long.

Colonel Lichel disappears, and Colonel Kessel takes sole command of the office. He speaks almost no Polish, and Olga struggles to maintain the charade that she doesn't know what he's talking about when he calls her a "filthy Polish cunt." Or has her type the caloric rations for the general populace and another for those in the ghetto. Or how to reinforce the mines on the bridges spanning the Vistula. She tries relaying as much as she feels safe doing to Father Matusik, but one Saturday, Mr. Tomkalski's oldest boy is waiting outside the confessional. He gives his head a swift negative shake and ducks behind the heavy curtain. Olga's relieved—she's being dismissed. Maybe the Resistance feels she's done her part. Or maybe whatever she's supplied has been so useless, they can't be bothered with her anymore. She doesn't care. She just wants to get home.

Then, the ghetto erupts in an uprising, and Colonel Kessel's fury rages. "Kill them! Kill them all!" he screams into the phone. Olga knows things, important things, but she has no one to tell them to. The ghetto is destroyed, and all summer Warsaw smells like smoke. In August, the heat is so bad Olga opens the window and inhales the scent of ash. At night, she holds Joy and prays, "Oh God, take me. Please let me be with you." Even while she sleeps, she listens for a knock on her door.

Winter comes again, and one evening she slips on a patch of ice, ripping the elbow of her coat and, worse, breaking her wrist. Unable to type, she's assigned to the filing pool, something she can barely manage with her sling. Again, Klara finds her. "So, Olga, got any more chickens?"

"What about the one I gave you?"

"Ate her six months ago." One of Klara's front teeth is missing. Through the gap, her tongue flickers like a sea creature tossed by a gray tide.

Olga thinks she should kill Joy, cook her, and give part to Klara. In the pockets of her coat her hands clench as if they're wringing Joy's neck, but she knows she won't do it.

"So, I hear you're filing now," Klara says.

"Yes. My God, how they love paper, lists, and then lists of lists."

"But papers have information." In front of the bakery Klara stops short. "Here, every Thursday, on your way home, buy some bread. There'll be a loaf waiting for you."

And so it begins again. The first three weeks, she has no information—she's been filing nothing but reports about the currents of the Vistula. Then, in April, she comes across a report on the availability of train cars to evacuate German troops from the collapsing eastern front. She shoves it up her cast, brings it to the baker, and leaves with a loaf of bread. The next week she brings a similar report on the availability of ambulances. When her cast comes off she's afraid she'll have to work for Colonel Kessel again.

But he's been replaced by someone who's brought his own typist from Germany, so Olga stays in the filing pool and tries memorizing a report on targets for likely sabotage, but terror so grips her mind that she can't even remember half by the time she reaches the bakery.

The park has become a wasteland, stripped of all trees, bushes, and benches. Even its encircling iron railing is gone. Nothing remains but a few streetlamps. A spring evening, and Olga sees something strange hanging from one. She senses that every step is bringing her closer to depravity's handiwork, but she cannot stop herself until she stands under it. Stands under a light pole strung with a sack of flesh. That used to be Tomkalski's boy.

With the bravery and sorrow above her, Olga's mind uncouples from her body, floats away so that it won't have to grasp what her eyes see. Or know what her own soul feels: how that hanging sack could have been her. She crosses herself and wills her feet to move. But she cannot control her bladder. It leaks all the way home.

She sews her father's books into the lining of her coat and starts sleeping in her daytime clothes—when the knock on her door comes she wants to be ready. One night, it does. She grabs her coat, puts it on, opens the door. Mrs. Tsarchuk's grandson stands in the hallway. "Go to the baker's. Go now!"

She glances at Joy. "Give her to your grandmother." The morning's curfew has another thirty minutes, but she manages to get to the baker's and is startled to find Old Pozwit behind the counter. Before she can say anything, he presses his finger to his lips and leads her to the basement, where he moves aside three tubs of lard and pries off a manhole cover—no wonder the old man always smells like the sewer. He motions her down. As soon as the crown of her head is below the surface, he replaces the cover, leaving her in darkness.

Someone takes her hand. Then someone else. Her eyes adjust, and she can make out figures. Some with weapons. Some without. The Warsaw Uprising has begun. She surfaces near the Vistula and someone hides her on a barge. That night she and others are ferried to Warsaw's outskirts. They need her to translate German intercepts. She tries, but isn't very useful. She's turned to stone with terror. She envies the others their rage. How their white hatred has superseded their need to sleep or eat. How they live to kill. For killing, they fight like drowning men struggling for the surface. While she sinks like a lump of coal.

By late September, it's clear that the Russians will not cross the Vistula to come to the Uprising's aid, and she rips the lining of her coat and takes out her father's German vocabulary. Beside "victory" she reads, "Winning and losing are artificial constructs, yet humans slaughter each other for their sake." And she knows she can carry on no further.

But she does. When the Germans begin their final, systematic destruction of Warsaw, someone takes her back to the sewer. She'll stay down there for weeks, surfacing at night to scavenge for food—a rat is a feast. Then the Germans retreat for good and the Russians secure their lock on Warsaw. A cruel peace.

They send her to a camp outside of Warsaw. And then to another, where she's processed and identified for what she is: a simple Polish woman.

When she's finally freed to find her way home, nothing but rubble remains of her building. She starts across the park. When she reaches her mother's building, she finds the front wall has been blasted away. She looks up and four floors above sees her mother's burled walnut cabinet teetering at the edge of air.

The wall supporting the stairwell has been blasted away as well, and the stairwell, stripped of railing and wall, is exposed. But Olga must go up. She must harvest some little thing, anything, from her mother. But the higher she climbs the tighter terror grips her. At the second floor, she starts using her hands like an infant and wishes she'd left her coat down below—it's bulky and snags as she crawls. She's almost to the third floor when her crucifix swings free, its chain catching on her chin, but she can't loosen it—she needs to keep both hands on the stairs.

Someone calls to her.

But she's too frightened to look down to see who.

Again, "Olga!" She makes herself look. Klara Kushka.

"Olga, get down!"

But Olga looks up at the burled walnut cabinet. Maybe she could find a cup. Maybe even a teapot. Just something to remind herself of who she had been before she became what she is: a woman in a ratty coat crawling up an open staircase.

But Klara keeps calling and she won't stop—Olga knows that much about her, so she starts down, perspiring and cursing her bulky coat and wishing Klara would stop saying, "Take your time . . . take your time."

When Olga reaches her, Klara grins, takes out a pack of cigarettes. "Want one?"

"Why not?"

So, they sit side by side on the rail-less, wall-less bottom step and smoke. Two women. Younger than thirty. Older than time.

I Want to Teach Camille

Jessica McDougald

Build yourself like one builds a house.

With your own two hands,
build the house out of love and reinforce
it with joy. Nail it all together with confidence,
keep extra in your toolbox.

Build a house you call
Mine.

It takes work to maintain this house—
there will be days you'll have blisters on your palms
and your muscles will quake in exhaustion
from holding up load-bearing walls against
hurricane force gusts of bad-days,
but you are strong, my girl.

Don't you know you come from a long line
of women with splintered hands
and houses still standing?

Don't you know that your veins pulse
with the grit of the Matriarchs?

Don't you know that your Mama and your Gram
and your Great-Nan, and your Great-Great-Grandma Hall,
and on and on until the Greatness becomes too much to count—
Don't you know that these Matriarchs kept their sheds stocked
with spare faith just so they could share with their daughters
when the walls began to lean?

We are women who are prepared
to defend the houses we built
against doubt's dry-rot, we are prepared
to stuff our prayers and all of our other certainties
at the threshold of the door when the cold
threatens creeping.

We are prepared to point the shotgun,
passed down by our Great-Great-Greats,
the one our mothers taught us to load
with bullets of our own self-sufficiency,
at the doors of our houses
when those who wish us harm,
those who want nothing more than to see
our houses smoldering,
light their matches and try to break in.

28 Days

Alyea Pierce

For 28 days:
This earth is red, and I want church.
This red earth is cemetery, and I want ceremony.
This red earth cemetery is the Sea, and I want baptism.
I want reverence and ritual;
dipped fingers bathed by blessing water,
bent knees at the pew,
and the sign of the cross,
giving praise to all four edges of this world black folk created
   communion.

I want removal of shoes and
washed hands before entering this temple.
I want Black women in white with
arched backs and open arms in offering
circling the gates of this red earth; protecting this red earth with drum,
   rum, and kreyòl chant.

I want remembrance beyond body.
Beyond this black body's step, song, speech, and swag
because these bodies who remembered how to make
home from hulls of ships,
music from iron,
and fight from force
deserve every honor in death.

Climbing the (White) Ladder to Success

Leeanne R. Hay

MY FAMILY HATED ME BECAUSE OF HOW I MADE A LIVING. MY NEIGHBORS IN the quiet building in Dallas, where I had resided for over ten years, were not-so-quietly working to have the condo board association force me into selling. They were not vague in expressing their desires for me to move far away. It seemed that dutifully tending my terrace garden and living a peaceful, single life was not quite good enough for them either.

Consequently, on a crisp Sunday morning with summer nearing its abandon to fall, I sat reading a real estate website for homes in the Garden District of New Orleans. The sunlight through the open terrace glass doors was changing to a softer glow. I caught a breeze with the scent of leaves no longer new. I couldn't help but look out and think back, the lyrics from a G-rated Disney movie as the background music in my head: *Shotgun shacks and mansions, Sugar barons and cotton kings. Rich people, poor people, they all got dreams. And dreams do come true in New Orleans*.

Ten years ago, the economy tanked. I lost my high-paying sales job because of a corporate reorganization where no one gave a damn about my stellar performance and loyalty. Two years later, I tapped into my initiative and started a business at my desk in the kitchen. Now I own a warehouse, have 100 employees, and do more than $250 million in annual sales.

You might wonder why my hard work and good fortune pissed off so many people. It turns out they don't outwardly like my customer base—even though some of them are a part of it. Behind closed doors and private mailboxes, my customers are addicts.

No, I am not a drug dealer. And no, again, I'm not trying to use some lame language to deny responsibility for being a drug dealer. And a third no to the presumed next question, "What, you sell bongs and other paraphernalia?" My customers think I am one talented marketer and often give me artistic inspiration. A few vulgar people and groups believe I'm the type of businesswoman who is leading society straight to hell. Tacitly, even more, people want to own my creations. They care little about the noise and revel in the puckish legend of how it all started.

In those long, lonely days after my unemployment checks stopped, I sent out over 400 resumes in a thirteen-month period of time that started in late 2009. I got two interviews and no offers. So, I began to take an inventory of what I did best and realized that I had been selling myself with the products I represented—and not in the biblical sense. My extensive research and dedicated knowledge of each customer's business needs (and their customers' wants on down the retail channel) were unwavering. I had made it easy for my customers to do business with the family-friendly (and internally bellicose) Crazy Crown Company where I had worked for over twelve years.

Having brought over $120 million in sales of party products to those corporate assholes, they decided I was no longer necessary because my territory was locked up tight under contracts (that I had won) for seven years. I had sold myself out of the job that another rep (a longtime drunk and notorious yes man) would then inherit to manage day-to-day issues—and get my commissions.

Joblessness created nervous anxiety in every waking moment, but I found fleeting inner solace with Reece's Miniature Peanut Butter Cups. I had to have the miniatures because of the quintessential peanut butter-to-chocolate ratio. And while grieving the loss of a job I loved, shit like this was absurdly necessary. Wearing worn-out sweatpants was important too. At the height of five foot eight, you can gain ten pounds and your clothes will still fit. When you spend nearly eighteen months eating your feelings of inadequacy and wearing what my mother would have called "trash picker clothes," you can pack on enough weight to bloat up to three dress sizes. Welcome to my chubby world.

My lackluster family's interest in my financial hardship was met with Depression era–like advice to "just go knock on doors because exposure could bring an opportunity." When I reminded them that "People die from exposure," they stopped calling and sending inspirational cards because, "Really, dear, you're getting to be so bitter about life. Maybe you should be more grateful. And it couldn't hurt to drop all that weight you've gained." Right.

Adding to my hermit-like existence was a total lack of exercise and general grooming that I used to take for granted. My shoulder-length haircut had grown long and straggly down to my boobs. The once golden-flecked highlights in my chestnut hair showed eight inches of roots, and I had neither the money nor the desire to perform any self-maintenance. All emergency funds were gone. I had traded in my one-year-old Lexus sedan with a note for an eight-year-old one with no payment. My next step was to take a desperation job (like working in a shopping mall food court) or get a grip on making an income to support myself because no one else was volunteering financial assistance.

Looking in the mirror one morning, I gasped and said out loud, "Jesus, look at you!" as the horrified face staring back at me was wearing a stain-smudged sweatshirt with my jiggling jowls. I followed it up with my customary internal war cry against a business competitor, "Fuck 'em." I was fed up with being sorry for myself and tapped into the unmitigated anger I felt. Then I resorted to doing what I knew I did best and committed to making money for the only company I could trust 100 percent—mine.

I had to get my professional appearance together. It was time to kick my own ass before others. I won't lie; this was the first of many battles with myself, and that first clash was the hardest. I had to exercise *in public* because I couldn't afford a private trainer. A local recreation center is a demoralizing place to work out among your neighbors when you need to lose a ton of weight and look like crap.

Nevertheless, I put my headphones in, climbed onto a treadmill, and hoped that if I kept my eyes shut, I would be safe in my playlist of old-school R&B hits blocking out any pseudo-social interaction. Along with "the gym," I knocked myself back to eating a daily 1,500-calorie, low-carb diet. I resigned myself to the fact that fiscal solvency and looking good trumped prurient enjoyment.

At the same time, while I was sweating my ass off, I needed to think about where to find a limitless market. What could I sell with a contagious excitement that would make enough people want to tap into it? On a stinking treadmill was where my research initiative started. My head was getting back into the game. At home, I would end up on the webpage of yet another webpage—you know what happens when you stray-click on mindless shit while wandering on the internet. It was the last click that would be the first step I took to create my company when I landed on Etsy.

Etsy is an online marketplace for small, independent artists and craftsmen. If you make glittery hair bands for preteen gymnasts or middle-aged transvestites, Etsy is the place to post your products for sale because it appeals to a younger and eclectic crowd that buys one-of-a-kind, handmade stuff. Have you just discovered your love of blowing glass into Christmas ornaments? Make a few distinctive samples, photograph them, and then post them on Etsy. Custom-make each one to order, and you have no cash tied up in inventory. Your customer prepays you before you spend one cent on materials. Also, there is a rare and elusive customer personality who shops on this site. Etsy customers have incredible patience because they appreciate and seek out craftsmanship in the unique products they buy. Sales and manufacturing on your time frame with others' money for someone broke is the ultimate business cash management concept.

I was working hard toward the packaging of myself as the frontline salesperson of my company. I had found the platform to launch it. Now all I needed was the product that would rock a little piece of the world for sales. And then for one dreadful moment, everything came to a standstill.

Richard, a former colleague of mine, had died of an accidental prescription drug overdose. I was shocked and saddened. However, I was not surprised.

A hard partier for many years, Richard's lifestyle was a true-life urban tale. At six foot three with the Black Irish coloring of dark hair and eyes and creamy complexion women envied, he was once an attractive and charming man. Great at sales no matter what the product, each year as his successes increased, his habits did as well. Even when his closest friends and I suggested that his pharmaceutical cocktails were like a contest juggling razor blades where a winner was still a loser, he didn't want to hear about it. When family and friends gathered for the last time with Richard's corpse as the guest of honor, there were few tears.

After his funeral, some of Richard's nearest and dearest gathered at his favorite dark and overpriced bar to lift a glass in his memory. While I picked at the spicy nut snack mix the bartender had set out, some of the others split a few white ladders to go with their drinks. And that's when it hit me. Almost everyone I knew from anxiety-ridden high school kids to my stressed-out middle management friends, to my great-auntie—they all had a prescription for Xanax.

If you have never seen Xanax in its original form and are being held hostage to the generic, alprazolam, by an insurance company that doesn't see the beauty in name-brand goods, fear not. The most popular size of Xanax, the two-milligram tablet, is a miniature work of art. The rectangular white tablet is scored with perpendicular lines in between each letter of its name: X|A|N|A|X. Stand it up on end and it looks like a tiny white ladder—hence the street name used by those who partake regularly.

So, there I was nursing my one glass of house red while the rest of the group were so mellowed out they didn't even care that their bar bill was pushing into four figures when they ordered their fifth bottle of Perrier Jouet champagne to toast our old colleague who had relaxed right into the grave. I didn't understand their nonchalant attitude toward mixing substances; they all thought that I didn't appreciate the stress in their lives that necessitated downing prescription pills with booze.

What I did understand loud and clear was that they all thought there was an ultra-cool vibe to their behavior. And people who were willing to spend this kind of money to keep up a persona would buy anything that promoted that façade to their group of peers.

What the 1990s had done for the style of "heroin chic," I saw in that bar the new style market for this decade—the *FanAddict*. This ever-growing group of people looked out at the world with glazed-over eyes and dreamy smiles. They saw themselves as an enviable caste adorned in their wraithlike fashion and accessories. And any group that was this stupid about the safety of their health was probably also self-indulgent enough to buy anything to vindicate their behavior—and share it with friends.

I left the bar early and walked home alone. I felt filled with an energy that I could barely contain and nagging knife-like thoughts poking at my conscience. My head was pounding with an internal argument.

The Still Silent Voice said, "It's wrong, what the hell's the matter with you?"

The Seductive Murmur purred, "It's perfect. You know you'll make a fortune."

The Still Silent Voice shushed, "People will make you out to be a drug dealer and killer who preys on the weak."

The Seductive Murmur hissed back, "Fuck 'em; you can't pay next month's mortgage."

Guess who finally won out?

I opened the door to my one-bedroom condo, dropped my purse, shoes, and jacket and pants on the floor. I walked straight over to my desk and sat down in my best work outfit—a T-shirt and panties. With just the overhead lamp turned on, I stayed there for over eight hours with my tools for war—drawing pads, multicolored sticky notes, pens, and pencils. When I realized I had to pee, the sun was coming up. As I got up and started walking to the bathroom, I looked back at my desk. The concept drawings of a unisex fashion line covered it—everything from fabric designs to jewelry and accessories.

From tiny white ladder decorative buttons for shirts to flowing fabric prints for clothing—I found the chemical makeup of alprazolam was an elegant geometric design. Extracting pieces of the molecular composition, I created patterns that would be printed in various colors and overlaid with an aesthetic nuance paying tribute to the drug that over 50 million people were swallowing every day in the US ("not counting worldwide users," whispered the Seductive Murmur). Designs were covert; in fact, these pieces could be an addict's private communication, an inside joke among their social behavior alliance.

I decided to fabricate jewelry for the first sample pieces. With small round and long tube silver-colored beads strung in a specific order, the design represented the Morse code dot-dash concept. The pendant charm spelled out *Xanax*. The complimentary dangle earrings with five beads each spelled *white* and *laddr*. I could make it in sterling silver, 14k gold, or platinum and encrust the dots with diamonds or another favorite gemstone. Clients could adorn themselves while advertising very private preferences. I could convert any pharmacological favorite into an understated announcement or invitation.

For my start-up, I had to make a set of photography samples from cheap materials until I got those initial prepaid orders in. I also knew that the biggest and best group for market testing was only a few blocks from my home in the small consignment boutiques of the nearby gay-borhood. If the chic boys wore it, the hot young waifs would follow. Then the rest of the ripples of teen fad cliques and middle-aged suburbanites desperately seeking one last grasp at a youthful persona would spend their money like a Juicy Couture tidal wave.

I fell into my bed and slept hard for ten hours. Then I got up, showered, and dressed for the day in jeans that hadn't fit in a few years and a little cotton sweater that showed off hard-won curves. For the first time in so many despondent months, I looked almost like my old self. Silently, I promised to get to the hairdresser as soon as I received my first payment for a sale. I left my condo and got in my eight-year-old Lexus sedan to drive over to the local craft store where a buffet of silver-like beads and findings awaited me. For the time being, this was the only source for materials I could still charge to my last credit card.

In three days, I made twelve samples with digital photos that I took with my iPhone. My next-door neighbor, Matthias (a laid-back musician living off royalties from his 1980s hits), helped me with photo enhancements and uploading the pictures to my new Etsy store site. I thanked him for his help and promised to make him a batch of his favorite brownies for payment as he walked to my door to leave. Still an easygoing '80s dude, he said, "Cool, sounds good."

As I was closing the door behind him, Matthias stopped, turned around, and said, "You know, I'm going to a party tonight. I could wear some of your stuff if you wanted."

I wanted.

Even though Matthias's last hit song had been almost thirty years ago, there had been a renaissance of sorts with middle-aged fans paying to download his music on throwback satellite radio stations. His label, always looking to milk every dime they could out of their artists' catalogs, often invited him to keep the parental gatekeepers of their nubile pop singers entertained. Matthias gladly obliged because "record label appearance checks still cashed, and the food and booze were free." Having never gained a pound and graying in a silver-fox fashion, he looked like a distinguished version of his former bad-boy self. "Cougar candy, still with a taste for the tender young ones who are getting harder to convince," he once said.

No one could have predicted what was going to happen that night at the party. But to this day, I swear in the recesses of my mind I heard the Seductive Murmur utter, "Rock 'n' roll time."

Less than twenty-four hours later, my FanAddict Twitter and Instagram accounts blew up. Some freelance paparazzo had gotten photos of Matthias wearing my necklaces and bracelets. While hanging on his recording label's hot, eighteen-year-old pop star, Matthias's one hand was copping a feel while the other was draping a few of my necklaces over her head. A tabloid TV news website had gotten a quote from Matthias about him "being a huge fan and addicted to her music, so I gave her some FanAddict jewelry."

It went viral.

My virtual store crashed Etsy's host site. They forced me to move my domain to a new host that could handle the traffic. Hello, Amazon.

As more publicity was generated about the new, irreverent designer who was "glamorizing prescription drug usage," the longer people would wait for delivery of my products. From a segment on a national news show about my "meteoric, yet controversial rise" in the world of fashion to a religious organization's documentary demonizing my company and me (which continued to endear me to my family and neighbors), every week brought at least one raised eyebrow from me. I still occasionally wondered how in the hell did all this happen?

Nevertheless, it did.

I no longer struggle with the disgust in the eyes of those who once claimed to have only my best interests at heart while I continued to disappoint them. I had reconciled myself to the fact that when I could barely keep a roof over my head, their response was to abandon me. Hence, some relationships hadn't changed all that much.

Now I just needed to finalize the purchase of a new home, then schedule the movers to take me to New Orleans—a place with a long history of not intertwining sound business judgment with public morality. Perhaps I might have an opportunity to expand my corporate interests there. An online business website I regularly read had a short piece on a particular party goods company recently falling on hard times from poor management. I smiled knowing that the cosmic bitch, Karma, was sending me good juju, as they said in my soon-to-be new hometown.

Before long it would be time to advance to the next rung as I climbed the (white) ladder to success.

Hercules

Anil Classen

SAMIRA KNEW THAT THE ROAD TO A HAPPY MARRIAGE WAS NOT GOING TO BE AN easy one. She had been told on numerous occasions by her bent-over mother that the road was a long and tiresome one. It would test her, make her question her sanity and turn the world on its head at times. And what for? For love? Her mother had laughed out loud at the prospect, as if someone had told her they had just discovered the holy grail, only to use the chalice as a drinking cup. Samira knew all this and yet she felt bound to follow the codes of conduct that her parents had instilled in her, the wheels already moving without her knowledge. There was little she could do to stop the engagement to a man she had only met briefly, a tall and quiet man who looked at her once before being distracted by his group of friends at her cousin's wedding. His look had said all she needed to know. *You are not pretty enough.*

"He's just shy."

Words a mother uses to soothe her child. Words that placate, a quick and simple solution to calm the fears of someone who does not know better. Samira had no experience to draw on. She was not schooled in the adult game of courtship. She knew nothing of the idiosyncrasies that men like Ismael carried like an armor. She felt the rebuff and her confidence had taken the knock to heart, the bruise forming involuntarily.

"You shouldn't have cornered him like that . . . in front of everyone."

Years later, Samira would see that sentence for what it really was. It was nothing more than her mother's usual tactic of turning the blame squarely on her daughter, illuminating the mistake so that every pore could be seen, the truth ugly in its entirety.

But she could not lay all the guilt at her mother's door. She had allowed herself to be swept up by the preparations, seduced by the detailed stitching on her gown, the white fabric so heavy, she had looked at her sister in desperation when she had tried it on for the first time.

"Don't be a baby. Yours is far lighter than mine was."

It was meant to make her feel better, but the tone had silenced Samira. She had looked at her reflection in the tiny room she was allowed to use for her fittings. Those television shows where the bride stood in a large room surrounded by her sisters and best friends were the material of fantasies, spun on American liberal notions. She had to contend with a badly lit room that had the luxury of a tall mirror that was in desperate need of a good clean.

As Samira looked at herself, her hair meticulously hidden behind a piece of tightly bound cloth, she saw her cheekbones take on new definition. Her eyebrows arched to newer heights, as if the lack of hair that normally surrounded her face acted as a distraction, drawing attention away from her large eyes that shone despite the lack of light.

"Stop posing so much!" her sister moaned from the doorway. "Do you want to try on the peach one? It has a gold paisley print on the border."

"No. The white is perfect," Samira said as she ran a hand across a silver-stitched peacock whose yellow rhinestone eyes peered up at her almost cheekily. It was so beautiful that she forgot why she was actually there. The pattern of flowers and peacocks was so intricate that it resembled the type of wallpaper she had seen in an ancient Mughal temple, one she had visited with her parents when she was much younger. She could still see the red stone building and the way the late afternoon sun had turned all the rooms into a mirage of blush tones, the endless decorations blending into each other as the heat level sank, announcing the mother-of-pearl light of the early evening.

Samira had stood in front of a portrait of an Indian princess, captivated by her bridal dress, the oversized nose ring immediately catching her attention. It was a statement, something that was surely uncomfortable to wear, but an adornment that made the face of the pretty young woman take on a sheen of maturity, and sexiness.

"There is no need for you to wear a nose ring," her mother snapped as they shopped for her wedding jewelry. "None of the women in our family have ever worn one. Don't you want to stick to tradition?" her mother asked accusingly. "What will I tell the people if they ask me why you have chosen such an adornment?"

Tell them it's my bloody wedding, so they should mind their manners and not ask such questions.

Samira should have said that, but the words lay in her mouth like angry breadcrumbs. Her tongue had felt dry, not agile enough to put force into the rolling bowling ball of anger in her head.

The wedding had flown by in a flurry of activity, dresses, and exhausting smiling coupled with rosewater-soaked almonds that her uncle had flown in especially for her. She had made it through the orchestrated posing for her photographs with half her dignity intact as her mother watched from the sidelines, clucking at every wrong move like an orchestra conductor. On her first night alone with Ismael she fell asleep almost immediately when he turned out the bedside lamp, and every night afterwards she turned onto her side, away from him and the possible affection that was her right.

"Time is a rolling marble that cannot stop itself."

Her mother's words stung, the statement plunging a greedy dose of poison into her flesh to first paralyze her and then wait for the inevitable. Five years flew by without her realizing it. Five years of birthdays and pretense. In five years Ismael had never once said he loved her, his routine taking the third chair at their communal dining room table. Samira shared him with his father's shoe business, busying herself with running the home and visiting her mother. She could not fault Ismael for the loveless marriage. He could not help it that he did not love her any more than she could help herself from pressing her face into her pillow every morning and screaming into the goose feathers after he left for work.

After two miscarriages, she had given up on having children. It did not help matters that her sister was pregnant for the third time, her body almost snickering at Samira whenever she saw the swollen belly under her tight tunic. She should have felt nothing but happiness for Jamiela, but there was no joy left inside her. The last miscarriage had been so severe that she had to be hospitalized. Her mother had visited her with a gloomy and almost angry face, telling her indirectly that this "whole business" was a huge inconvenience, throwing out her schedule. Samira had closed her eyes to the green eyes, seeing only the accusation there. *You have let us down yet again, Samira.*

"I am going to leave him."

Her sister had looked up from her knitting, her pregnant belly looking almost comical under a roll of thick green wool. Samira did not have the heart to tell her that the idea was awful. No child should have to wear such a dreadful color, even if the jersey was made with love.

"What are you talking about?"

"Ismael."

"Stop being silly, Samira." She sighed, openly annoyed with the drama landing on her doorstep. "Do you really think you can just leave him? Just like that?" she asked, snapping her fingers in the air.

Samira bit back the disappointment. It was difficult under the glare of the fluorescent kitchen light where every detail was magnified, sparing nothing that was meant to be hidden. She had hoped that her sister's first reaction would be to take her in her arms and ask her why. That would have been a reasonable reaction to such a statement, surely? Was her happiness that insignificant that the first reaction was an announcement about what she couldn't do?

"No, I mean it."

The stony silence felt overwhelming at first, but then it became so unbearable that Samira stood up, almost toppling her chair over.

"Is that all you have to say? Wow."

"What do you expect me to say? You simply throw in the towel and I am meant to pat you on the back? Is that what you want?"

"It's been five years, Jamiela. *Five*."

"Do you think that has anything to do with my response?"

"It should."

"You're going to break Ma's heart. You know that, right?"

"God!"

Samira could hardly bear the sight of her sister anymore. She just sat there, with the knitting in her lap, with her proud stomach on display. How could she imagine what it was like to be in a marriage where there was no communication? It was all a farce, a wonderful game of pretend that was woven around Ismael presenting the perfect husband in public and Samira the doe-eyed and docile little wife. When she had told him about her plans to enroll in community college, he had remained silent. The only sign that he had heard her was the tightened grip on the newspaper page that was held up blocking his face from hers.

"Ma will never forgive you for dragging her through the shame of a divorce."

"I expected more of you, Jamiela. I did. I guess I am the fool here. You have not even asked me why. That would . . . should be a question that you ask your sister when she tells you that she is planning on leaving her husband."

"But—"

"I should have had a brother."

"Why?" The annoyance almost curdled with the wounded pride Jamiela tried so hard to push away from her pretty face. She had always been a stubborn sibling, swallowing her pain in gulps, her smile too forced, fooling no one.

"Because he would have at least cornered Ismael. He would have forced him to make a stand, not like you—"

"What have I done wrong now?"

"You should be on my side, Jamiela. Can't you see that? You should be the one cornering Ismael. Only you sit here and think of—"

"What?"

Samira sighed loudly, sounding like an older version of herself, a version she was set on avoiding at all costs.

"You are only worried about what other people will think . . . instead of what I think. That is so . . . awful."

Samira turned around and walked out of the kitchen, past the toddler who was playing in the lounge on the maroon circular rug. She walked out the front door and into the street, almost directly in front of a car that was seconds away from crashing into her. The loud hooting stopped her before she burst into tears for all the world to see.

Had Jamiela asked her why she was leaving Ismael, she could have told her the precise moment when the lining had finally torn in her marriage.

That day, when she had returned earlier than expected from her grocery trip, the howling kettle on the stove had masked the sound of her key in the door. Ismael was already home and, for once, Samira did not call out to him as was her habit when she returned home. She liked the sound of the kettle, insisting they buy it when they moved into their house. Samira's mother had one of these, a reminder of her homeland, the whistle of the kettle transporting her to low roofs and tiled floors where the women of her family spread their cooking utensils before them, not at all inconvenienced by the lack of modernity. They had been preparing meals this way for centuries.

"I can't just jump whenever you tell me to."

The sentence made her stop in the hallway that was landmined with creaking floorboards. One false step and her cover would be blown.

"I can only come tomorrow when she is at her mother's . . . yes . . . around three."

Samira felt the air constrict in her throat to such a degree that it became painful. She had been holding her breath, convinced he would hear her if she opened her mouth. The only sound was the kettle being lifted off the stove and then the sound of a metal spoon landing clumsily on porcelain. Then the sentence that would change everything, a string of words that could have been used anywhere in the world and would carry a totally different meaning.

"I love you."

It was the declaration that she had been waiting for, the words that only one person could say to make the sacrifice less demeaning. Samira had waited for him to smile at her like Jamiela's husband, with a tenderness that made words unnecessary. What were words anyway, but the spoken feeling we could not show? Ismael saying this to a stranger, someone he had chosen over her, was the crack in the surface that now ran quickly, spiderwebbing the smoothness of their relationship, robbing the light of its chance to glimmer off their time together, despite both of them knowing it was far from perfect. The unspoken words had taken on a magnitude, a force that he could clearly shower anyone else with, except his wife.

I am enrolling at college. I am fed up with being the only unhappy person at the table.

She looked at the car that had almost knocked her over and resisted the urge to slam a fist on the metallic red hood. She took the bus to the registration office and smiled at the tired-looking lady behind the counter as she took the large folder of information into her hands. It felt heavy, but then again, everything worthwhile always did.

"EVERYONE IS TALKING ABOUT you going to college."

Her mother was standing with her back to her, bent over the sink as she cut the bad parts off the green beans she had bought at a discount store. Samira knew that this was a cheap trick, fooling foreigners like her mother into buying vegetables that technically should have been thrown out the day before. Her mother, like all the women in her neighborhood, felt thrifty as they pushed the browned vegetables toward the cash register, their eyes glowing as the pound price flashed bright green before their eyes.

"They have little to talk about then if me going to college is making waves."

"Cheeky!"

"What did you think they would say? They would never think to support someone furthering their education."

"Isn't being a wife enough for you, Samira? That husband of yours . . ."

"What about Ismael?" she asked, dreading the end of that sentence.

"He is being very generous, allowing you—"

"I need his permission?"

"He is your husband, isn't he?"

This was the tactic Samira's mother always used. She answered questions with more questions until it frustrated her daughter to such a degree that she gave up, allowing the argument to disappear like the end of a fireworks display, the sky dark afterwards, making the fireworks almost appear imagined.

"Why can't you just be satisfied with what you have, Samira?"

There. That was the moment she knew that her mother was no longer the person she could rely on. She would have to forge a way around the moat that surrounded the castle of her dreams. She would have to find another way in, past the alluring candy-coated happiness her marriage was supposed to bring her. She had to ignore the pull of expectation, the way things had always been, never questioned because it was rude to ask why. It was frowned upon to want more than what had been dished onto your plate, a meal you had never even asked for.

"Is this what you really want for me, Ma? Do I look happy to you?"

"Happiness is a luxury. A luxury that your generation seems set on having, come what may."

"And you don't want that for me, Ma?"

"What I want is inconsequential. The Almighty has his plan. It is up to us to honor that."

Three tough sentences delivered with a bluntness that punched the air out of her. She still had a hunger for something more, a hunger for something that would fill her, make her sit up in the middle of the night because she felt happiness instead of the hollowness, the lack of all that she felt missing.

"I choose happiness, Ma," she said, looking out of the window and into the yard where two boys were kicking a faded yellow soccer ball against a wall with a surprisingly accurate rhythm. "I choose happiness."

"Well then you will have to choose it over duty, my child. Happiness always comes at a price."

"HE'S BOLIVIAN. I THINK his name is Julio."

Samira looked into the blue eyes of Sarah, her one and only real friend.

"What?"

"I said, he's Bolivian." She rolled her eyes for further effect. "You have been staring at him for two weeks and nothing! Not a *hello*, or *how are you* . . . not even a smile in his direction," Sarah said with open exasperation, her pretty face lighting up comically as she pretended to mirror Samira's coquettish behavior.

"You are—"

"I am not imagining anything. You *have* been staring at him. You know it. I know it and chances are he knows it as well."

"I have not been staring. You are terrible. You are too nosy for your own good," Samira clucked, turning her eyes back to the open book that had to be read by the end of the week or else there would be hell to pay.

"I am all of the above, but I am also a master of observation, you see. God, Samira, you need to just smile at him. He has noticed you. I have seen him watching you when you walk into lectures."

A smile. What a simple and almost noble concept, Samira thought. She had not smiled at a man since her wedding. Her scarf shielded her from most men trying to look at her, the cloth acting as a repellent, something that no westerner dared to look at too long out of fear of being politically incorrect as well as insensitive. Samira knew that most men believed she was pious and god-fearing, her long hair tucked so severely away that they were left to imagine what her hair looked like, a fantasy she was sure many men in her course entertained as they watched her pencil notes into her textbook.

"It's been over six months. You are allowed to live again, Samira."

Sarah was her only friend at college. She had spoken to Samira on the very first day, bridging that awkward gap, saving Samira from having to navigate the seating in the lecture hall and the dreaded lunch break in the cafeteria. Sarah had no idea what this simple act of kindness had meant to someone like Samira. She had only noticed the lost look and had wanted to help. Samira almost cried when Sarah offered her an apple at lunch, an act so selfless that it made her wish they had met earlier, but in the past she would have been surrounded by Muslim girls who watched her every move, weighing up her behavior for comment and later ridicule when they returned home to their curious mothers.

Sarah was also the first white girl Samira had ever shown her hair to. It had happened in the safety of Sarah's restroom, after Samira had accidentally spilt coffee over her blouse, an act that made her feel stupid, even though she was not to blame. The perky waitress behind the coffee counter had not been paying attention as she slipped a lid onto the piping hot coffee cup. As Samira slid her long sleeve over her head, her scarf came undone, revealing the mass of curls that sprung loose, surprising Sarah.

"I was not expecting . . ."

"So much hair. Yes. I guess not." Samira laughed as she turned away from her friend.

"Can I ask you something?" Sarah asked, her voice lower than usual. The change in tone made Samira nervous.

"Sure."

"Why do you . . ." The hesitation made Samira feel embarrassed for her. "Why do you cover your hair?"

It was something Samira had always dreaded. This politically loaded question that always said more than the question demanded. It said that she was unable to be proud of something as intrinsic as hair. It said that she was hiding something that the world had every right to see. To "cover" automatically had a bitter aftertaste, something that was tied to shame, even though someone like Sarah would never be able to grasp the deeply tied tradition and pride that she carried within her whenever she tied her hair up, sliding the scarf over her head, shielding her beauty from the world like a secret only few were privileged to see.

"Out of humility," she finally answered, looking into the mirror as her friend eyed her with a bit of tension in her eyes. "I know that a lot of people don't understand it. They think that I am a slave to my religion."

"A slave is a bit harsh."

"But the truth often is harsh, Sarah. It can be downright blunt when it wants to be."

"I didn't mean to offend you," she said as she turned around. "I just wanted to know."

"And I didn't mean to be blunt," Samira offered, turning to look at the back of Sarah's head as she pretended to look for something in her bag. "Sarah?"

"What?"

"Do you think I should cut it?"

THE HAIRDRESSER WAS A friend of Sarah's. She looked like a punk rocker, her three lip piercings sparkling slightly, distracting Samira as they discussed possible styles. Had she not smiled sweetly, Samira would have bolted, running down the street like a madwoman. Instead, Louise, who had been at school with Sarah, chatted rather nonchalantly about hair lengths and possible styling methods.

"A choppy bob . . . yes," she said as she ran her experienced fingers through Samira's thick hair. "It will look amazing with your bone structure."

Bone structure. Samira had never used the phrase before, and suddenly she found herself moving her face from left to right, watching how the light fell on her cheekbones.

"Are you up for it, darling?"

Samira looked into the mirror and caught the wink from Sarah.

"It's your call," Sarah said as she took a seat in an empty chair at the next mirror. The salon, a mix of retro collectables and too much chrome, made Samira think she had wandered in by mistake. Where she normally cut her hair was nothing like this. The salon all good Muslim women used was tucked away, hidden from the street because no passerby had the right to see these naked heads on display. Instead they were curtained off; the only natural light was a sliver of clear window glass close to the roof where occasionally you could see the British sun attempting to cut through another embankment of light gray clouds.

"Are you ready?" asked Louise as she combed Samira's hair backwards, tightening it into a ponytail. "I can't glue it back on once I start cutting." She laughed, stopping herself when she saw the serious face that met hers in the mirror. There was no room here for lightheartedness. Samira had never had a drastic haircut. Her mother had always sat beside her as she had the ends trimmed, the full mane of curls springing in all directions, much to the annoyance of the Muslim hairdresser who never smiled. Samira always wondered if the hairdresser ever wanted to do something out of the ordinary, instead of coloring hair and snipping off the dry and unhealthy bits. Was she happy doing routine maintenance, like a car mechanic servicing countless engines?

"Okay. Here goes."

There was the delicate sound of the scissors applying pressure to her hair and then a lightness that followed, surrounded by silence in the salon. Two women sitting behind her had turned around in their swivel chairs to take in the moment. Their eyes grew wider and then, as if it was a normal progression, their lips formed into shocked, happy smiles.

"Yes," murmured Louise behind her, before she turned Samira's chair around so that they were face to face, but it was pointless. Samira's eyes were closed.

"Don't you want to see it?" Sarah asked, the joy skipping in her voice like a child hopping on large stones across a river.

"It's not that bad," encouraged Louise.

"Not that bad," screamed Samira suddenly as she opened her eyes, to be greeted with a cheeky smile and a hand holding up a tied piece of hair. Louise looked like a Red Indian holding up a prize piece of scalp.

"I'd reckon around thirty-five centimeters."

"Wow. You could donate it, Samira."

"Yes, you could. There is a flyer at the till, if you like. All you need to do is fill it out."

Samira pushed her face into her hands, surprising the two women, who looked at each other with questioning eyes.

"Samira, are you okay?"

Silence. The other women turned around, realizing they were invading Samira's personal space.

"I think she just needs a moment," Sarah offered as Louise slid her chair slowly away. "Samira, look at me, please."

But her head remained down, tucked into two palms that wedged them securely, stopping any outsiders from seeing her face.

"I think you are going to be surprised if you just open your eyes and see the length. It's only the start of your haircut, Samira. Trust me . . . and Louise," she said, winking at her school friend.

Samira took a deep breath and pulled her hands slowly away from her face. When she finally looked into the mirror, she saw the sliver of light between her hair and shoulders, the strands flying slightly as her head turned from side to side.

"Let's get this show on the road," Louise murmured as she slid her stool closer to Samira. "I still have a bit of work to do here," she said as she started pinning sections of Samira's hair into position.

There was no way for these women to realize the step Samira had taken. They were used to walking into salons and taking control, allowing magazine pictures and hairdressers' advice to guide them toward a new, polished, better version of themselves. When they were children, they could tell their parents what they wanted in bold, unmistakable tones that made them sound mature for their age, something most mothers were proud of. Samira was never indulged that way. She had only one duty and that was to sit still in the hairdresser's chair or risk her mother's wrath when they returned home. There was no room for discussion about new lengths or a "feathered" cut, the look of the time when she was a teenager. She could not talk about braiding her hair, or even changing the color. She had to be content with a simple cut, her tongue lame in her mouth, angered by the obedience she offered without debate.

"All right, I am done. You can look now," Louise said nervously as she took a step backwards.

As her vision shifted into focus, Samira saw the new length and the way the curls now stood differently because they were weightless. She saw the almost playful movement as she turned to look at Sarah, who was pouting cheekily, waiting for a reaction.

"Well? Oh, for god's sake, Samira. Will you say something? Louise is dying inside, poor thing!"

She looked back at the mirror and ran her right hand through the hanging curls and shook her head as if she was trying to shake something out of her hair. Then she looked back at herself and up into the eyes of Louise.

"Thank you," she said, her smile spreading slowly. "It's—"

"Fucking awesome!" Sarah yelled, slapping Louise on the shoulder. "God, Samira, you look amazing!'

One of the women who had turned around earlier shot Samira a smile in the opposite mirror.

"It's only hair," Samira said in a lowered voice.

"No, it's far more than that, silly," Sarah said as she hunched down so that they were face to face. "It's a new start."

"YOU WERE THE ONE who wanted to go out dancing and now I'm the one waiting for you."

Sarah stood with her hands on her hips, her hair tied up in two buns that made her look like a grownup Minnie Mouse. The rest of her was serious, her cat's eye makeup harsh against her pale skin that looked almost milky in the dull light of her bedroom.

"I will only be a minute," Samira called from the tiny bathroom. She stood there, staring at her reflection, watching her new hairstyle move as she shook her head lightly. The freedom she felt around her shoulders felt unreal in the harsh glow of the bathroom. She knew that there was nothing she could do to bring back the hair that was now gone, except wait for it to grow back. But she knew that she would never allow that to happen again. She would now visit a salon that welcomed her with a smile, with a store window facing the street for everyone to see her as she sat there having her hair styled.

"We are going to be late."

Samira nodded at the mirror. In the end, she had decided against donating her hair. She had been thankfully spared the interrogation from both Louise and Sarah as she slid the ponytail into a plastic bag. It felt wrong to leave it there, in the hands of someone she had just met.

"I will just be a minute!" she yelled, shutting her eyes for a second before she lifted the lipstick to her lips. As the color spread across her skin, she was surprised at the transformation. She looked at the fullness, the luscious hue that sprang back at her. She resisted the temptation of blotting the color off. She would wear a bright color tonight. It was time to celebrate.

"I just need to make one stop before we go out to the club."

"Will you come on, already?" Sarah moaned, even though her focus was on Samira's naked head, the scarf neatly folded and left on the bathroom sink.

"Are you ready?"

"Yes." Samira smiled as she slipped the brown carton into her bag and caught sight of herself in the full-length mirror on the wardrobe door. The tight-fitting dark blue jeans and tight black T-shirt made her feel exposed. She was suddenly unsure of herself. Was it too much?

"You look fine."

She turned around and looked straight into Sarah's approving eyes.

"Who would have thought . . ."

"What?"

"That you would be the vain one!" She laughed as she opened the door.

As Sarah bought a packet of cigarettes at the small shop around the corner, Samira walked toward the back and handed the package to the student with too many pimples behind the post desk. He looked at her with clear disinterest and gave her the till slip without comment.

"Do you want anything?" Sarah shouted from the front, ignoring the frown from the shop owner who clearly wanted order in his little shop. He hated white girls who thought they could do as they pleased.

"No, I'm good."

That night, as the music lifted in the overcrowded club, bodies heaving against each other, Samira felt claustrophobic under the neon lights. She saw Sarah at the bar and stopped herself from walking toward her. She wanted to stay in the middle of the dancefloor. She wanted to feel the push and pull of the crowd as they swayed to the electronic beat. She wanted to close her eyes forcefully and forget the lost hair, the past that nagged at her all day long. Samira wanted to push her fingers into the air like all the other girls around her and close her eyes, allowing the music to lock her in the moment, shutting off the voices that told her she was wrong to want this life.

"Here's your drink," Sarah said as she squeezed her way through, making space for herself in the crowded area. She looked up at the DJ and threw him a big kiss. This was Sarah in her element, the lightness of her spirit so intoxicating Samira almost envied her, but she knew better. She knew that envy was a futile emotion. No one really knew someone's story and Sarah's was far from perfect. She deserved to be this free.

"He's at the bar."

"Who?"

"Julio."

Samira raised an eyebrow that was now visible because a series of lights flashing across the dancefloor had lit up her face almost spectacularly.

"He asked where you were."

"You're lying."

"Well, if I am, then why is he looking at you now?"

Samira looked over Sarah's shoulder and there at the bar, leaning with his back against the metal-topped bar stood Julio, his hands in his jeans pockets, watching her intently.

"You should go over."

But Samira was not focused on him anymore. She was closing her eyes as the music soared above her. She was thinking about that package she had posted and the route it would take until it landed at the right address. She could see her mother looking surprised at the postman as he handed it over, her face too shocked to tell him he had the incorrect address. Samira could see her close the door and then lock it, shuffling down the hallway and into the kitchen where she would be undisturbed, the space her father rarely walked into. Then she would slit the cardboard open and look inside, not thinking to look at the sender address on the bottom. Her curiosity always did get the better of her in the end, but this time the contents would stop the anticipation in its tracks. There, cradled in white tissue paper, her mother would find the ponytail, the last part of her, the part she needed to rid herself of to feel the world crack itself open, revealing a spectrum of color she could never have imagined.

"He's coming onto the dancefloor," Sarah said, before turning her back to the bar.

"Then let him," Samira said, surprising herself, the tone new and strong.

As she lifted her hands to the ceiling again and felt her hair falling away from her face, she already knew he was behind her. She did not need to turn around to be certain. He would wait for her to turn around and look at him. She kept her eyes closed and danced, the rhythm taking her away, shaking the fear from her like an old skin that she no longer needed. And then she felt his hand graze the side of her, telling her to turn around finally, to look at him because, like her, he had been waiting for something to start and burst into technicolor life.

Phoenix

Thea Swanson

I've thought to thank my adversaries. They told me they loved me while they mapped my demise. They led me to the hot bottom tiptoeing away, my brain sizzling, body limp, my children I forsook. When the deluge smashed, they, who weighted their crafty intellect as scarce as palladium, suckled standby fatherly teats or stumbled through rubble, mind muddled. I stood erect, wits clear, purveyed gray landscape and shed man-made skins decades worn. A dormant creature emerged, beholden to no one. She felt her pulse. She examined her phalanges, her tibias. She cracked her knuckles and rejected all labels. She would please herself and her charges, the kernel of her being rubbed raw and ready. Look, there. She runs miles, metatarsals touching down times thousands. See her shoulders, bare to the sun? Free of the yoke of history and liars? Songs in her ears not dirges buoying her burdens but electric rhythms carrying her past the sludge of men. One day, these millennia will be named days of the veil. But look now. How she beats the ground. How she soars.

In Love

Vlada Teper

The theater in *Santiago de Cuba* opens its mouth—
long, wooden plank teeth
suck us in every morning.

We are not here to watch.
We are here to meld.

From inside, the world is a
gaping hole with trees.

From inside, we stretch
towards the ceiling,
move beyond our dimensions,
toward the infinite,
the intimate.

Willing our pelvises to move first,
we will our snake selves, our swan selves
into being.

We are Elegua,
the child God
holding the Guava stick, then,
swapping it for a
machete,
we knock obstacles out of the way.

Moving across the wooden planks,
pulsating forward,
we become rumba,
clean the floor and get vacunao-d,
the sweat making our bodies sparkle,
washing us over,

so that by the time we
hold hands in a circle during *rueda*,
we are swimming together,
through heat, desire, lust, war,
in love.

Choices

Pamela O'Hara

AN ELDERLY WOMAN HOLDS A SIGN READING, "WE WILL ADOPT YOUR BABY."
The word "We" is underlined and highlighted in pink, though she
stands alone. I suppose she is the early bird of the group. I work
nearby and often see four or five protesters with their dead fetus
posters standing on that corner.

Though the woman's face is hidden, I'm sure she's tracking our
progress as I drive past her and turn into the clinic parking lot. Tall
green screens mask a chain-link fence and shut out the "normal" world,
the sunshine world, the mundane careless and casual world. Inside the
fence feels more like a prison, darker, a bit threatening; I'm tempted to
turn around and park farther down the street, across from the juice bar
with flower boxes, swinging ropes, and frozen fruit drinks as a reward.

"You good?" I ask Shannon as I turn the car off.

"I'm good," she replies, a little too fast, searching with her
fingers up and down the car door trying to find the handle to open it.
"I don't know how long it will take, but I can call you."

"No, I'm coming in." I pull my own handle open so she sees
which silver panel she needs to reach for.

As soon as we are out of the car, I regret my parking decision
again. The only way out of the fence is across from the clinic entrance,
which means walking past Lonely Poster Lady. Between gaps in the green
screen, I can see that she's still there paralleling our progress across the
lot. I reposition so that I am between the woman and Shannon.

"Please don't kill your baby," she shouts louder than she needs to as we round the corner out of the privacy fencing. I recognize her immediately as Nurse Barbara from church, the same Nurse Barbara who has helped me with the scrapes, splinters, and various booboos of my Sunday school students over the years. When she recognizes me, her lips snap shut to hold in the startled cry.

I didn't realize I had stopped walking until Shannon tugs me forward.

"Wait, please. I will adopt your baby," Barbara offers more kindly, pointing to my belly.

I can only imagine she feels betrayed to see me here. Of all the people in this oversized college town, I regretfully run into my favorite grandma from church. We've discussed her pro-life views, but I'd not pegged her as an extremist. I once stayed up late into the night at a women's retreat arguing the finer points of the medical versus moral definitions of the start of life with her. She educated me on the timing of the formation of a zygote, I educated her on the social, economic, and health benefits of choice. I came away from the conversation feeling good that we could discuss our fundamental differences based on facts and logic and without descending into ugliness. But there is no time for intellectual discourse today.

"I will take care of your baby," she offers again.

"It's not that easy," I think but do not say out loud. I slow my pace to block her so that Shannon can continue inside. I nod to Barbara in recognition, apology, and warning as Shannon walks into the building. I turn and follow.

I'm still thinking of lonely, committed Barbara an hour later as I hold Shannon's hand, seeing the pain on her face.

"It hurts too much, I can't do it," she whimpers, with no option for undoing it.

I had not realized there would be this much pain. I suppose taking a fetus out of a woman's body should, evolutionarily speaking, be unbearable. But it surprises me that in a scrubbed white room with devices beeping and drugs dripping, there is not a way to lessen the distress. Probably a lawmaker somewhere decided that this is a pain that must be felt.

"I can't," she begs.

"I'm here," I remind her.

I'm here because another doctor in another scrubbed room with devices beeping and drugs dripping birthed me. He had intended to wrap me up and carry me off for some loving family to adopt, as was the way with unwanted pregnancies back then. But my mother changed her mind. She chose to keep me and love me and give me all the advantages that allowed me to get married, have three kids of my own, and be here for my young friend in her moment of need.

This choice is not an option for Shannon.

"UNDIAGNOSED CHILDHOOD POST-TRAUMATIC stress disorder," Shannon had read to me from the pink and white floral notepad I had given her to take notes at her psychiatric consult. One week after the pregnancy test, two weeks before the clinic visit, we sat in the same car in a different parking lot to figure out how to take care of Shannon.

"Well, duh," I wanted to say, but knew that would not be helpful. Did it really take modern attitudes on mental health to recognize that witnessing the tragic death of both parents could shatter the emotional development of a six-year-old child?

"I need to experience my emotions," she continues to read. I lean back in the driver's seat waiting to hear what other insights she has gained, but she looks up, ready for my response.

"What else did you learn?" I ask, shifting my body in her direction, purposely not starting the car so she knows she has my focused attention.

"That's all," she says, glancing down to make sure she has not missed anything. "I need to experience my emotions," she repeats.

"Oh." The word hangs there by itself for longer than it should. I force a reassuring smile and relax my shoulders so she doesn't feel my tension. Two days of consults, two weeks of waiting, just to learn that their conclusion is what I already knew at the introduction. I should have lied and said I was family so I could ask more questions.

"Oh," she echoes then seems to remember, "I need to see another doctor."

Of course. I forgot medical science no longer involves one doctor, one diagnosis. It has become a rabbit hole of referrals with more ruling out than ruling in of data points from different specialists.

"Did they set something up for you? Do you have a name?"

"They will call me next week to let me know which doctor I can see, and I can make an appointment then."

"Did you tell them about the appointment at the clinic?" I ask, knowing that the termination will add more trauma.

I can tell she didn't share that. "They will call me next week," she restates. "I asked her what time they'll call because my shift break is at eleven. I can't take a break before then unless I ask my supervisor. She wa . . . wa . . . wa . . . wrote down eleven." Her stutter reveals her anxiety.

"Good. That is very good," I reassure her. "It's okay if she calls early because you can always call her back. I am so glad they are finding someone to help you."

I know this is just the beginning of a long journey to break the cycle of low self-esteem, abusive relationships, and self-harm, but I am impatient to get help. Professional help from smart people who will know how to help Shannon take care of herself. I thought when they heard the enormity of the situation they would expedite the process. But I guess many situations are enormous and many people need help.

I realize that the groans have stopped and the room has gone quiet.

"Is that the end?" Shannon asks me or the doctor or God, I'm not sure which.

"You may feel some cramping as your body rids itself of the placenta," the doctor explains. "It should only last a few hours."

"She'll have contractions?" I ask incredulously. "But she didn't give—" I stop myself.

"Her body doesn't know that," he apologizes, pulling off the rubbery gloves and signaling the nurse to start the cleanup.

I had thought there would be a recovery room, but before long the nurse is handing us papers and signaling it is time to go. Glancing at Shannon, I can tell she is not ready to leave. Her eyes are closed and she has curled up on her side against the bed rail. When she opens her eyes, I see she is still crying, out of sadness or pain, I am not sure. I help her up and we slowly make our way back through the office and out of the waiting room.

As we exit the building I see there is now a crowd of protesters, but no sign of Barbara.

"What did your baby do wrong?" one of the protesters screeches as we pass.

"What if your mother had killed you?" another voice screams.

"You are a strong, brave woman," I tell Shannon, raising my voice to drown out the protesters. I want to move faster to get past the tormenting, but Shannon is too fragile. Her steps are slow, as if she is trying to move her feet without jarring the rest of her body.

I see Barbara approach, offering Shannon another arm to lean on. The elderly woman starts humming a tune I recognize, but can't identify.

"I am woman, hear me roar," Barbara starts singing louder than usual. I smile, recognizing the old hippie song.

"In numbers too big to ignore." I join in, understanding the lyrics will drown out the ugliness of the crowd.

We make our way slowly past the crowd, Barbara and I singing to each other across Shannon's hunched form. Once we are in the protection of the raised fence, the shouting ceases.

"Give her a heating pad when you get home," Barbara advises me. "If she starts to run a fever, even low grade, take her to the ER. You can call me if you have questions."

I'm not sure how to respond to the generosity of her caring.

"I was an OB nurse," she explains. I guess she still is.

"Shannon, this is Barbara," I introduce. "She goes to my church. She takes care of broken children," is all I can think to say.

I'm not sure Shannon hears me, she's more focused on moving her feet forward toward the car.

"Shannon," Barbara whispers gently, reaching so that she holds Shannon's hand in hers. "Would you like for me to adopt you?"

Shannon looks at me and I reply, "We'd love that. Thank you, Barbara."

Exonerves

Lisa Fransson

IT'S A STRANGE THING TO GO TO BED IN ONE CITY AND WAKE UP IN ANOTHER. It's a strange thing to arrive at a house in a forest, where a receptionist hands you a key to a room and tells you to enjoy your stay, as if you belonged there. And it's a strange thing that such a house should have a shared lounge and a shared kitchen, where people greet you as if they already know you.

"Evening," said a man in a pixie hat pulled down low over a graying ponytail, who sipped milky tea from a saucer. "Where've you come from then?" he asked.

"London," I replied and pressed the button on the kettle. I'd been thrown about on the sleeper and as soon as I'd arrived, I'd changed into my softest pajamas and bandaged up my hands.

"London?" said the man as he poured more tea from his mug onto the plate and slurped. "Poor lass," he said, shaking his head.

I sniffed my chamomile tea—it smelled of weedy garden paths. "I'm here to spend time with trees," I said. "Only," I turned around to look at him, "I'm not used to them."

He put down the saucer. "Trees?" he said. "I suppose they make good company." He frowned and scratched his scalp through the hat. "Yes, I'd certainly miss them if I had to do without them."

I nodded and stirred my tea. I understood exactly what he meant. When I'd first been alone in my room here in the forest, I'd found myself struck by the lack of traffic droning in the background as if by a violent blow. I'd begun hyperventilating and for a moment I'd thought my entire nervous system was about to detach from my skin and crawl off like some giant stick insect, back onto the sleeper and home to my flat in London.

"So," I said and sat down opposite him, holding the mug in my bandaged hands. "What method of approach would you recommend?"

"Eh?" he said, looking away from my hands to meet my eyes.

I smiled and waved. "It's nothing to worry about. Just exonerves. I've been prescribed trees. That's why I'm here in this," I swept my arm outward, "countryside."

"Exonerves?" he said and leaned forward, squinting to get a closer look at my hands. "Must be a London thing," he said.

When he leaned in like that, I could smell the wind on his hair, the sun on his skin, and the earth on his clothes—and at that moment, I desired to possess that smell more than anything. My hand shook as I lifted the mug to my lips.

"I expect it is," I said. "A London thing."

"And spending time in the forest will cure you?" he said. His half-full saucer stood pushed to the side.

I nodded fiercely. "How do I start?" I said leaning forward, eager to learn. "What do I do?"

"Well," he began as he leaned back in the chair and pushed the hat farther up on his forehead to scratch his hairline, "getting into the forest proper would be the first step."

I nodded again.

Now he flicked his ponytail. "There are plenty of good walks. Maps should be in the stand on the reception desk. You can do short circuits, middling circuits, or long circuits that take all day. And that's about it."

"Really," I said.

I must have sounded disappointed, because he leaned forward again, clasping his hands on the table. "Trees don't expect much from you. That's the best thing about them."

"Of course," I said and smiled. "Thank you." I stood up and held out my hand for him to shake, but he just stared at it until I began to feel awkward.

"Wouldn't that hurt?" he said.

"Ha!" I said and withdrew my hand. "The pain would have been excruciating."

THE NEXT MORNING I sat on the sofa in the reception with my brand new walking boots laced up over cushioned plasters, gel insoles and extra-soft walking socks, and the map spread out on the coffee table in front of me. I knew about maps: maps of flight routes, the insides of aircrafts, and airport landing strip systems. For the sake of dexterity, I had removed the bandages and was instead wearing gloves. With the tip of my finger hovering just above the paper, I traced the longest route around the forest, climbing up the hill for the first half and then turning to travel back down into the bowl where the youth hostel stood for the second, as I mouthed communications to an imaginary version of myself, already out there, scurrying ant-like along the path through the trees: "sixty-seven kg, long route cleared, November Echo, estimated at six hours, ready for take-off."

On the floor stood my daypack stocked with water, oat cakes, and dried bananas. The weather was glorious, the sun beating almost too hot through the window, and the air so still I could have trapped it in a jar. Yet, I remained sitting on the sofa with my finger poised over the track. From time to time I glanced up as other people wandered through in ones, twos, and threes, their leather-creased, mud-spattered walking boots fused to their feet, carrying backpacks that had molded themselves to their shapes. "Morning," they nodded, and I nodded back.

The flow of adventurers eventually tapered off. I folded the map, placed it in the outer pocket of my rucksack, and walked over to the receptionist, who was about to pull the shutter down for the morning.

"Excuse me," I said.

She halted with her hand on the shutter, and I braced myself for the usual impatient smile. But, "How can I help?" she said as she let go of the shutter, sat back down, and rested her elbows on the desk, as if time was hers alone.

"I was wondering about the man in the kitchen," I said. "Have you seen him this morning?"

"Which man would that be?" she said.

"He was in the kitchen last night," I said, "drinking tea from a saucer. He had a ponytail and a hat."

"Hmm," she said and swiveled on the chair to face the computer where she began tapping the keyboard. "I wasn't on duty last night," she said tapping a few more keys. She leaned toward the screen, squinting at some sort of table. "We're pretty chock-a-block. This weather," she said turning back toward me and waving her hand at the window. "People are flocking in from the cities."

"He's not from the city," I said. "He knows about trees."

I must have looked desperate, because she offered me a pen and paper and said, "Tell you what. Write your name and number here. I'll be pottering around for another couple of hours and I'll keep an eye out."

I held up my gloved hands. "I have a problem using my hands at the moment."

"Oh," she said. "My granddaughter suffers terribly from eczema. See if you can get some sun on your skin while you're out there today."

I was about to correct her, but instead I just wiggled my raised hands and smiled back at her. Because maybe sunshine was the cure? Maybe my nerves would recede back inside my skin, so that I could go back to work in the tower. But no sooner had I thought about the tower before I gasped in pain, even the soft fluff on the inside of my glove chafing. I turned from the desk and sort of billowed my arms around the rucksack. The contact caused agony, but I counted my steps as I walked outside, where I sat down on a bench by the wall to take extra slow control tower breaths until the pain receded; I wouldn't remove my gloves just yet.

Two hundred meters down the road and to the right was where I turned onto the path. So busy was I, first taking out my map to double-check directions, then confirming with the wooden sign, triple-checking I had my water bottle, and finally trying to follow the route in my head as it had looked on the map, all the time glancing behind me, in case a pixie-hat would come bobbing after me, that I didn't notice the trees—suddenly they were all around me.

There were no trees on landing strips, or anywhere in the airport. Nor did trees grow underground, along the tube line. Were there trees on my walk to the station? I'd never noticed any. But then again, in London, tree-gazing would be a death-defying sport. How easy it was to get hit by a black cab, or a bus, or a cyclist, or a motorcyclist, or a kid on a scooter, or a swarm of language students. Anyway, they would be city trees: stunted in growth, leaves coated in dusty grime, with poisoned sap.

Now.

These trees.

Here.

In this forest.

These trees were.

Majestic!

I leaned my head back as far as it would go and turned on the spot. Above me the crowns spun, so tall that I could not see the tops, only a tapering off as if the treetops pierced the very sky. How come planes didn't fly into them?

"Because," I said to myself, "planes cruise at an altitude of thirty-five thousand feet and these trees are maybe twenty feet, pushing thirty at the most."

Still, what a bewildering perspective to be on the ground looking up. I pushed my hair away from my face to take it all in.

Then there was the smell, like organic all-purpose cleaning fluids, only fresher. I had an urge to remove my sweater to let this air soothe the skin on my arms, but everywhere was rough bark and protruding branches. To snag a nerve—without a doubt I would unravel.

I crossed my arms and hugged myself. "Trees," I said. "Just what the doctor ordered." The path lay ahead of me, inclining upwards, and there was nothing to do but to place one foot in front of the other, for the next six hours. I looked once more behind me before I sighed and took a step.

After an hour or so I discovered that there wasn't much to this walking. Just keep lifting my feet and make sure not to trip. The trees seemed at moments a solemn, straight-backed crowd, gathered especially to watch me walk past. This made me nervous and eventually, to break the ice, I picked one that grew close to the path, its roots bulging upwards under my feet.

"Hello," I said.

"Nice forest you have here," I said.

"My name's Avery," I said.

"I'm out for a walk," I said.

"I'm an air traffic controller," I said.

"At Heathrow," I said.

"I work in a tower," I said.

"It's eighty-seven feet tall," I said.

"So, quite a bit taller than you," I said.

"Not that it's a competition," I said.

"But I expect planes aren't your thing," I said.

"All that pollution," I said.

"In the air, in the water," I said.

"To be honest," I said, "I think I may have gone off planes myself."

"There was a storm," I said, "the day the plane crashed."

"The timing of that lightning made it so much worse," I said.

"Even I, for an instant, thought it caused the crash," I said.

"But the pilot had misprogrammed the flight management computer," I said.

"She had some personal problems," I said.

"But that's irrelevant," I said.

"Because whoever controls the traffic bears the ultimate responsibility," I said.

"That's the truth," I said.

"The inarguable truth," I said.

"Inarguable," I said.

I had become too hot, but as I pulled at my roll-neck, the tree shed a needle that lodged in between the fabric and my skin. I gasped at the wave of pain racing through my nerves. As soon as it localized to the soft spot in between my collar bones, I carefully pulled my top away from my skin, leaned forward, and shook the needle out.

"Oh," I said after a while, breathing out. "There was no need for that." I breathed in deeply through my nose to stop the tears from gathering. "I was just trying to make conversation."

Why had I, a stranger in this forest, assumed I'd be welcome? Up until now there'd been birdsong. And the occasional sudden flap of wings rising through the branches. And a sort of continuous buzzing and shuffling. For a while the gurgling of a stream. But now the forest had grown silent.

A cloud crept in front of the sun, and I stopped to pull on a jumper against the sudden chill. The light gained a dusk-like quality— darker and darker, until the path in front of me resembled a grainy security camera image.

I calculated that I must be at the farthest point from the hostel, which meant that the way back would be equidistant to the way forward. I nibbled on some dried bananas for courage and drank a few sips of water, then I screwed the top on tight with my teeth before dropping the bottle inside my rucksack. Why had he, that oversized gnome with his hair and his hat in the kitchen last night, not said to bring a raincoat?

But I should've worked it out, shouldn't I? Because if trees ran for shelter, they would have abandoned London long ago.

I started to walk again. Above me, the clouds continued to pile on top of each other, pressing downward, and my exonerves warned of a rapidly lowering air pressure. "Just put one foot in front of the other and repeat," I told myself.

By the time the first heavy drop landed on my forehead, I was already taking great big strides along the path. Soon the rain spilled from the sky. I lifted my face to let it wash over me and I stood there, turning around on the spot, enjoying how it cooled my nerves without causing pain.

Then I shivered and thought that I'd best be on my way. But in this eerie daytime darkness it was difficult to tell which line through the trees represented the path.

I stood there, trying to remember any landmark that I'd walked past before I'd stopped, like a rock, or a stream, when the sky cracked in two. Such was the violence of the thunder that I dropped onto my knees. I hunkered with my hands covering my ears, until the force of the rumbling pushed me forward. My hands splashed in the mud as I caught my weight, and I felt the thunder roll along my spine. The rain was beating the dirt on the ground into a soupy liquid that swirled around my hands, and my clothes clung to my body. I raised myself back up on my knees and bent my head backwards to see the sky. Above me the tree crowns slotted together in a dark network. Only blotches of ragged clouds showed through the swaying, rain-heavy branches.

The thunder rolled away, echoing and murmuring into the distance, and I pushed myself up from the squelchy ground. The mud flowed around me, carving rivulets through the forest as it searched for a way down.

Wait!

I closed my eyes and remembered my finger tracing the route this morning; the path goes upward for the first half and then it travels back down for the second, into the bowl where the youth hostel is.

"In that case I shall follow the mud," I said and stepped forward.

Walking was no longer straightforward; my boots sank deep into the mud. For a while I tried to step from root system to rock to bigger root system, for a more robust surface, but I slipped on these as I slipped elsewhere.

Another thunderclap and I crouched by a lichen-covered boulder. My fingers curled into the crevices, wanting to hold onto something, only to grasp cold slime. I pulled my hand back to see chunks of putrid fungus smeared on the gloved palm of my hand. Flinging the glove away, I tried not to think of maggots and decay.

I rested my forehead against the rock, checking first that there were no more surprises. "My name's Avery Celandine and I'm an air traffic controller," I whispered. "I'm out for a walk." The rock felt solid against my skin. "I need to keep walking."

I stood up again, but my hand shook as I dragged it across my forehead. "Right," I said through chattering teeth while the clouds continued to collide above me. "Upwards and onwards."

For a while I thought I'd found a trail to follow; the mud snaked along, creating a small stream. But soon, as the trees grew closer together, the mud-stream narrowed into nothing and I found myself scrambling over rocks and roots as thick as my thighs. My sodden jumper caught on a branch and tore. I crawled backwards out of it and left it hanging on the tree. My heart beat faster and my breath came shorter. I stopped for a moment and held onto a tree, taking slow control tower breaths. "My name's Avery Celandine and I'm an air traff—"

An almighty crash and a blinding flash—I threw my arms around the trunk and screamed as a branch gashed my forehead. Somewhere near I heard the slow splintering of a tree falling. The air crackled and filled with the smell of burning wood. Lightning lit up the sky once more and I saw the fallen tree up ahead, split down the middle, smoldering on the ground, its roots reaching toward the sky.

And I saw something else too: the silhouette of a man, holding onto a root and standing with his head bent—a hat pulled down over long hair.

"Hello," I shouted. "I've lost my way."

But when I got there, there was only the fallen tree on the ground, the fresh wood on the inside of its split trunk glowing bright in the gloom.

"Hello," I said again as the lightning died in the sky. "My name's Avery Celandine and I'm an air traffic controller. I'm fit and healthy. I'm going for a walk in the forest." But I was shivering so much that each syllable came out garbled.

I slid down the trunk and sank into the soggy moss. The water seeped through my trousers. When I licked my lips, I tasted blood. Above, the thunder kept tumbling. I closed my eyes and saw the plane coming in for landing, the lightning striking the wing just as the wheels folded out, the tilt and the impact with asphalt, fountains of sparks from the friction and the engines bursting into flames. The pilot, Abby, burning in front of her screens as she turned toward me and said, "Get up and get out of the forest, Avery. If lightning strikes again, you'll fry."

I grasped a branch and pulled myself up. But now my remaining glove caught and tore. Another bang and a fork of lightning striking nearby. It must have been conduction, because a fury, such as I've never known, entered me. I gathered all the air inside my lungs into a scream, then I ripped the torn glove from my hand and threw it down. When I found that my boots were stuck in the boggy ground, I took another deep breath and screamed again, before undoing my laces, pulling my feet out, and marching off, not caring in which direction the mud flowed. My sodden socks sloshed through the sludge, until they also were dragged off and left behind.

Barefoot I stomped through the forest, pushing branches aside so forcefully that they whipped behind me and sometimes snapped. The endless lightning strikes showed my progress in horror-film snapshots: the contorted branches, the dormant moss-covered rocks, the watchful trees. If I fell and couldn't get back up, would they tear their roots from the ground and come scuttling to gorge on my flesh? "Well, I'll make it easy for you," I shouted into the storm as I stripped off in the rain, swinging my clothes I know not where.

"Spend time with trees, they said," I shouted as I tore and hacked and pushed my way through the forest, cutting a path where none had gone before. "So soothing, they said." And I hopped up on a rock and stomped down on it. "I don't know what kind of trees they were talking about, but it certainly wasn't you lot. Ganging up on me, causing this," I threw my hands up toward the sky, "turbulence!" I hopped off the rock and stamped the ground hard again. "Turbulence!" I shouted as I walked backwards. "That's what all this is. Sodding turbulence!" Then I turned and at that moment my foot landed on solid ground.

I paused. The rumbling faded, the rain slowed and fell quietly, gentle against my skin. Up ahead a familiar wooden sign pointed toward me. I turned toward it, and in my mind I was already sipping tea in that shared kitchen. The feeling of heat from the mug against the skin of my hands so real that I didn't notice him until I ran into him.

"Ah," he said, stepping back. He breathed in as if to say something else, but stopped mid-sibilant, frowned, scratched deep through his pixie hat, and looked me up and down, even leaning to the side to take in my profile. "You all right, lass?" he said.

"Never better," I said and shivered.

He unzipped his parka and hung it around my shoulders, zipping it back up. "When the storm broke, I thought I'd better pop out to find you."

I laughed. "The forest is huge," I said. "And every bit of it looks the same as every other bit."

"I got lost in London once," he said. "Couldn't tell one street from another."

"They have taxis in London," I said.

"Taxis, hey?" He held up my soggy torn jumper, then one of my gloves with bits of sludge hanging off, and finally a branch with a skein of my hair knotted to it. "All creatures leave tracks," he said.

I touched my scalp, fingers tapping, searching for a bald patch.

He flapped my jumper toward my hands. "How're those nerves of yours?"

"My nerves?" I said and frowned. I pulled the sleeves of the parka up, turning my arms slowly, taking in the scratches, the swellings, the bruises. "My nerves," I said lowering my arms, "appear to be fine." I shivered once more.

He took off his hat and pulled it gently down over my hair. "Trees must've done the trick then."

I touched the hat. The wind in his hair, the sun on his skin, and the earth on his clothes, I closed my eyes to breathe him in. "My name's Avery Celandine and I'm an air traffic controller," I said.

"My name's Énna Blackwood and I'm a forester," he said.

"I'm forty-one," I said, opening my eyes.

"It's a good age," he said. "I'm forty-six."

"That's not too old," I said.

"It's not," he said.

"It's getting dark," he said, putting his arm around my shoulders to steer me toward the hostel. "When we get there, I'll make you one of those yellow teas," he said.

I nodded.

"While you get some dry clothes on you."

I nodded.

"And then you can tell me how you found your way."

"How I found my way," I whispered and smiled.

Your Daughter Is a Full Moon

Sabrina Strand

The world does not need shrinking women,
starving women, women working hard to shapeshift into men, to
lose the curve, the padded flesh of womanhood.

What we need in this time of darkness is big light.

When a woman says no when her body is screaming yes,
a part of her spirit chips off, the size of
a firefly quietly blinking out.

The world does not need quieter women,
docile women,
women with a palm on their mouths playing a pretend game of
incompletion,
      but the wild wisdom of womanhood
rooted in abundance, in compassion, in love.

Women renew themselves by drinking deeply from the cup of pleasure.
Their souls expand like sponges in pleasure's pool.

When God made me, it was under a full moon,

And I came out grande size, filled to the brim,

Faith and passion spilling over my edges.

Why would I try to dampen a spirit big enough to illuminate the
world?

Your daughter is a full moon—round, complete, unquestionably
brilliant.

Don't you want her to take up space, to belong everywhere?

Why would you ever tell her to be anything less than full?

Free

Jacqueline M. Gryphon

i am the possum playing dead
    the mole who burrows under your devious manipulations
    the fox . . . watchful.
in the twilight i am the rabbit gone to ground, safe
    the firefly lighting my own way
        out of your reach
    the clam digging deeper into the beach
        where sand fleas congregate
            to witness my going and becoming.

a raven kronks and bobs delight that i have learned its calls and leaps
    and in my unbound dance unbroken
        proved the lesson, taken flight.

The Renovation

Vanessa Park

THE LANDLORD WANTED DANI TO MOVE OUT BUT SAID SHE DIDN'T HAVE TO. He wasn't equipped to be the bad guy in a situation like this. Dani had rented the tiny bungalow from him for twenty-two years. He'd been a genuinely shitty landlord, and he was fully aware of that awful truth. When he went over to tell her about the plumbing, he felt the weight of that guilt sitting like an iridium golf ball behind his eyes.

Not that he needed to tell her about the plumbing. Dani'd told him about it off and on for years. Not to mention that she could see down into the basement whenever she peed. There was a crescent-shaped sliver opening near the pedestal of the toilet that gaped slightly when she sat down. She had developed elaborate ways to crouch over the seat, putting her feet in different places each time to distribute her weight. She tried hard to avoid full contact with the toilet seat, and the envisioned inevitable moment when the whole thing would just crash through into the cellar haunted her.

She figured the chronic leaks that her landlord never fixed were to blame for the rotting subfloor. She figured he would come fix it if the toilet went into the basement, but she did not want to test that theory, in case he didn't.

The day he came by she almost didn't recognize him. She thought, as she peered through the crack allowed by the chain, "I haven't seen you for years, Mr. Tarantino." Instead she just said, "Hi. What's wrong?"

As she spoke those particular words, her brain was busy with incriminations and the usual inquisition, most prominently (1) You should have said it's about time you got here, Mike, and (2) Stern-face-not-scared-face-get-rid-of-that-scared-face-now.

She tried to adjust her features in obeisance to her inner voice, but it was hard to do the stern face she practiced in the mirror when she could not make eye contact with Mr. Tarantino a.k.a. Mike.

The landlord part of Mike's brain was already annoyed as shit. The basically-decent-guy-who-made-a-terrible-landlord part of his brain thought, "Oh, God. She's pathetic. How can I kick her out?"

"Hi, Dani. C'n I come in? I need to talk to you."

She stood there for three full seconds without moving as she thought through the possible outcomes of opening the door to him, not many of them very hopeful. Then she realized the outcome of not opening it would be nothing good either, so she stepped back and disappeared behind the door as she unchained it and opened it.

Mike walked through carrying two large paper parcels. "Your laundry was delivered. I found these on the stoop." He turned around to peer behind the door to where Dani still stood, uncertainly. "Let's sit."

The tiny house was one room, about 250 square feet. The kitchen was a fridge, stove, and sink, with about two feet of countertop, all bunched in one corner. Dani's big round kitchen table took up the end of the room nearest the compact kitchen. Her laptop was open, and a purple teapot sat beside a mug shaped like a jolly penguin. At the other end of the room, her tidy twin bed was draped in a creamy crocheted coverlet. In the middle, in front of the bungalow's best feature—a picture window looking out onto a small unmowed field—was Dani's chair, a coffee table stacked high, but neatly, with books and magazines, a floor lamp with beaded shade, and a bright red ottoman.

Dani walked into the middle of the room and looked at Mike. "Okay?" she said, but it was a question.

"First let me take a look at the bathroom situation." He dropped the two laundry parcels on the table and went to investigate.

The bathroom was the only other room in the house. A rectangular space, it was where Dani's only closet was, as well as a full-sized aqua blue tub, and an equally aqua blue sink and antiqued white vanity, faintly chipped. The tub and sink were spotlessly clean, as was every inch of grout between the mustard yellow tiles (Mike remembered his dad got those for free back in 1965). However, deep rusty stains marred the absurd blue porcelain. The shower head hung partly loose from the wall. He could see where Dani had tried to reaffix it with duct tape. He opened the door of the vanity to see a bucket under the trap for the sink. He turned on the water and understood why. All the water that drained from the sink gushed directly into the bucket. A finger poke told him all he needed to know. The trap pipe was totally rusted through. He groaned inwardly, which to his inner ear was a Gregorian chant of acceptance of his unworthiness: Fuuuuuuuuuuuuuuuuuuuuuuuuuccccckkkkkkkk. Fuuuuuuuuuckkk. Fuck.

I have no business being a landlord, he thought.

The toilet sat delicately balanced on an oval of cracked linoleum through which the subfloor was horribly visible, as was the basement below. "Dani, this is dangerous! You really should have told me about this."

She was outside the bathroom looking in at him through disbelieving eyes.

Suddenly filled with misgiving, Mike said, "You told me."

She nodded. "I emailed you." When Mike did not immediately respond, she went on. "Once in November of 2012 the first time I saw the basement through the floor. I waited six months and when you did not answer, I wrote to you again."

"That was three years ago." Mike was incredulous. At her patience and his assholishness.

"Yes, that's true." Dani turned around and went to the big round table. She sat down, waiting for Mike.

* * *

SHE LOOKED OUT THE window next to the table at the stockade fence that divided Mr. Tarantino's property from the neighbor. Sometimes she could see movement through the thin gaps between the boards of the fence. She knew a man lived there with his nearly grown daughter. When they moved in five years ago, they'd come and knocked on her door. She almost didn't answer. But Dani knew the difference between being careful and being rude, she really did. That's why she answered the door after all.

It had, of course, been awkward, as the neighbor introduced himself—Dylan Gladstone (or maybe it was Glenrock?)—and his eleven-year-old daughter. They'd moved from down south so he could be near his aging mother. He just got a job as a manager at the Staples one street over. His daughter (Dani couldn't remember her name) was in middle school at Red Clay Consolidated. Though Dani never opened the door more than ten inches, she did muster a smile at the little girl and said, "Welcome to the neighborhood."

"What do you do?" Dylan asked politely.

"I don't get out much," Dani whispered, as she began to close the door, inch by inch. "I work on my computer."

"Really? That is very interesting! What do you do?"

"Oh . . ." Dani looked down at the child. "Well. I write." As Dylan took a breath to reply, she said, "I should go," and closed the door, oh so gently.

Recovering from that interchange had taken the rest of the afternoon, but she was glad to know a kind man and sweet-faced girl lived next door. The house on her other side, sliced into four apartments, never seemed to have the same tenants for more than six months at a time. She pretended it wasn't there.

PRETTY SOON MIKE CAME to sit down at the table with Dani. He didn't talk to her about moving out. Her vacating was, indeed, his fondest wish. He could redo the whole house. Let his grown daughter live here. Or rent it for more money. Or just sell it. But he knew he would never evict Dani. Instead he sat with her that morning and explained that he was finally going to do something about the bathroom plumbing—the whole room in fact. But it would be a huge disruption in her life. He described the reality of a month with no shower, no toilet. She grimaced slightly throughout but only looked genuinely alarmed when he explained that every weekday there would be workers in the house. The bathroom would be gutted. There would be noise, dust, and people. But in the end she'd have a safe, clean, convenient bathroom. And they both knew that meant she would be in no danger of falling through the floor while taking a piss in the middle of the night.

Part of Mike wondered if all that truth would spark Dani to abandon hope and just move out, but he knew better. She had nowhere to go, really, and the one perk of renting from a crappy landlord was the rent was cheap.

Instead of saying she wanted out of her lease, Dani said, "Thank you, Mr. Tarantino. I am very happy." She did not ask if her rent was going to go up. It did not occur to her, as it had not gone up even once in twenty-two years.

TWO WEEKS LATER, CONSTRUCTION began. Dani had nowhere to hide.

The contractor met Mike at the cottage the first day. He asked Mike, sotto voce, "Are you getting a porta-potty for her?"

Mike nodded. "I'm going to look into that, yes. But the local general store already told me they'd let her use their lady's room whenever. It's just three doors down."

Dani sat in her chair, looking out the window, hearing it all. Speak up, her inner voice told her, scolding her: you are useless to everyone, even yourself.

Dani knew she'd never walk down to the store. Mike knew she'd never walk down to the store. But he felt better knowing she could. But he knew she couldn't.

* * *

AS SOON AS THE workers left at 4:30 that first day, Dani raced to the sturdy bucket she had pulled out of the basement. She squatted over it and peed like a racehorse, as her dad used to say. That was a long time to hold onto her water. There had to be another way.

DANI STOOD BESIDE HER table. Her laptop was open to speakupforyourself.com and her heart was crashing against her chest, her legs vibrating as fight or flight hormones squirted through her veins. She visualized it: picking up the phone to call Mr. Tarantino. "Mike?" she would say, assertively and firmly. "I require a porta-potty be put off the back porch for my use during construction. I don't mind sponge baths and washing my hair in the kitchen sink, but I deserve a place to go to the bathroom, don't you agree?"

No, that's not right. Don't ask if he agrees. It doesn't matter if he agrees. It could turn into a debate about the need for a porta-potty and it is not a debate, is it?

"I deserve a place to go to the bathroom, and you, as my landlord, are required by law to provide such."

There. That sounded really good. She walked to the door of the bathroom where one lone worker was laying freshly cut joists onto the sill where the new subfloor would go. She said, "Do you need anything?" shocking the hell out of him. He banged his knee as he fell onto it, looking up at her. He'd never heard her voice. Not once in seven days on the job.

"No, thank you, Ms. Drake. I'm good. Pete and Lem went to get some supplies at the lumberyard. We're fine."

Dani smiled a small smile. It hurt a little bit, but she liked the way it felt. She left by backing up until the man, also smiling (a bit awkwardly), turned back to his task.

Excellent practice, she thought. Now I can call Mr. Tarantino. Now I can call Mike.

* * *

Every night, Dani took her bucket into the back field, emptied its contents into a small trench she had dug, and tossed in some leaves and dried grasses. It had taken her over an hour of digging the first night, using a giant slotted spoon, to get a trench about ten inches deep and three feet long. The night air was damp and cool. The sounds of distant traffic seemed very close. A rustling in nearby trees was enough to send her back inside to peer out into the dark for ten minutes, waiting to see if anything, or anyone, was there. Finally it was done. She felt like a refugee, or a resistance worker, as brave as brave could be, every time she went out to her trench with her bucket.

The day after she talked to the workman but did not call Mike, Dani made her way the half block to the general store. They knew her there. They had a delivery service and Dani depended on getting most of her everyday items from them. She paid her bill at the end of the month and carefully tipped the delivery boy or girl two dollars every time.

When the owner, Clare, saw Dani standing inside the door, she smiled and beckoned to her. Dani moved cautiously behind the counter and into the alcove where the "employees only" sign on the door gave her a jolt. When Dani came out, Clare said, "How's the construction going?"

Dani had an answer ready for this question, and three others she thought Clare might ask. She cleared her throat delicately. "They are working very hard," is what she said.

Clare grinned. "I know it can be such a pain. We had our kitchen redone a few years ago at the house and I thought it would never end."

When Dani did not say anything, Clare went on: "Do you need anything before you go?"

"No, I still have everything. My next delivery will be—"

"That's right. You'll email us your list on Friday, is that right?"

Dani nodded and moved sideways toward the door. Just then a tall woman in a knee-length mohair sweater strode into the room, laughing into her phone. Before the door could slam shut behind the woman, Dani had slipped through it and was on her way. Clare called out, "Bye!"

THAT NIGHT DANI SAT on her back stoop—she thought of it as her back porch—when the sun went down. The air had an acid bite as the temperature dropped. Dani realized that the way the air pushed her hair off her neck was a memory of being a child, outdoors, falling through moment after moment in air that did not feel safe, but that captured her and made her want things.

The stockade fence between Dani's house and Dylan's property was about fifteen feet away. She usually avoided even glancing that way, fearing an encounter. She sternly reminded herself that there *was* a fence that *did* protect her from any unexpected meetings. How can you be afraid of an invisible person on the other side of a fence?

The sun had been down for an hour. Dani thought about that stupid damned bucket inside the house. She looked out at the small field behind the bungalow. A hazy gibbous moon shed enough light to see the blond stalks of old grasses bending faintly to the north as a breeze wafted through. Dani stood up on the faded gray planks of the back stoop and walked to the bottom step.

This time the adrenaline was nothing but exhilaration and the giddy surety that she was about to do something truly great.

She pulled down her jeans and panties all at once and stepped out of them. She picked them up and then stood with arched back and pissed into the night air. The sound of the stream hitting the grass was the best sound she'd ever heard.

Seconds later she was inside. The lights were off; the dark gave her permission to grin, and to walk half naked to the kitchen where she rinsed herself, patted herself dry with a paper towel, and washed her hands. Next time she'd have toilet paper at the ready.

Next time? her inner voice asked, sarcasm oozing. Dani kept grinning.

* * *

DYLAN HAD SEEN DANI outside more in the last two weeks than at any time in the last five years. Twice he'd seen her go to the store and come back empty-handed. It didn't take a genius to figure that one out. Dylan got a bead on Dani that day they met so long ago. He realized more in that ten-minute exchange than would make Dani comfortable, but what that meant was, he did not go there again. He had no desire to cause stress and misery to the poor woman.

He had admired her hazel eyes, rimmed with straight black lashes, and the very long, immaculately brushed dark hair that caped her shoulders. He only glimpsed the eyes twice as they talked, both times when she looked directly at Melody, his daughter. Her button-down men's style shirt had rolled sleeves and was tucked into belted, spotless Levi jeans faded almost white.

Melody asked him at dinner, "Why don't you just go tell her she can come here to take a shit? And shower too? I mean, wouldn't it be neighborly?"

Dylan tried to explain. "At least the store is neutral ground, or as neutral as any ground ever is for someone like Dani. If I offered . . . Let's just say, she is handling this the best way she can."

BY THE TIME THE third week of construction was under way, Dani was spending more and more time outside, after dark. Whenever she woke in the night, she stood on the edge of her back "porch" and peed into the grass. It made her want to whoop aloud, the very thought of which shocked her into meditative wonderment. Back in bed, she would lie awake for a while, thinking about the urge to make noise, thinking about her naked bottom, the darkly furred triangle where legs met torso—a place not even she had looked upon, let alone anyone else, since she was—what?—eight?

The moon was almost full. Her forays now moonlit, Dani felt sure she was not alone. The moon was her companion, joyful at Dani's wild abandon. One night after coming back inside, Dani crawled between her sheets without putting her panties back on, or her pajama bottoms.

This time, her inner voice was almost kind. See what you've been missing?

Yes, Dani thought, it feels very good.

IT WAS ON THURSDAY around midnight when Dylan glimpsed movement at Dani's back door. He had taken the garbage out and then walked for a bit, through the back field that abutted the houses and shops on this semi-suburban road. In the moon's silver glow, he saw a shadow emerge from other shadows. It moved away from the door and became a silhouette. The figure walked to the bottom step. What Dylan saw made no sense at all. So, he continued to strain his eyes to see who it was, even though he already knew. But then she peeled off her drawstring pants and he saw a shining stream of glittering moonlit piss arc shallowly away from her as she stood there, hands on jutting hips. "Goddamn." He whispered it. Out loud. And stared. With genuine admiration.

MIKE CAME BY TO see how the bathroom job was coming along. Dani opened the door before he knocked. She stood in the open doorway wearing black yoga pants and an olive-green long-sleeved T-shirt with *Al Gore in 2000* in orange letters faded to pink. Mike stood there for a second, uncertain. Dani said, "I heard your car."

She stood back to let him in and returned to her computer. He called after her, "I'm here to talk to Lem." She nodded and waved her hand vaguely as she peered at her screen and began to type.

She heard them going over things in the bathroom. The floor and wall joists were in, the sheetrock up, a new bathtub was in place but not hooked up. Their voices faded as she immersed herself in her job.

Here's what she did not hear: "She goes out twice a day now." That was Lem, in confidential tones.

"You mean she really does go to the grocery store?"

"Well what the fuck did you expect? You never got her a porta-potty for fuck's sake."

"Well you said you didn't need one."

"How is that relevant? You have a tenant!"

Mike cringed. "Yeah," he retorted, his whisper fraying at the edges, "but obviously she's fine."

"No shit she's fine. She makes great coffee too."

Mike left, genuinely perplexed.

IT BECAME A MATTER of urgency greater than any biological urge—to find a way to sit on the back stoop-porch with her computer. Dani stood in the middle of the room for a few minutes, thinking. She glanced around her space. She bit her lower lip and then got moving.

One of the chairs from the round table worked well and was an obvious solution. After it was out there, she looked down at it for some time, then out at the field, then she rolled up the sleeves of her paint-spattered plaid yellow button-down shirt.

Next, her red ottoman came out. Next, a Rubbermaid bin full of old journals. It had been in her closet, but along with all the rest of her belongings was now part of a neat stack beside her bed. The Rubbermaid went on top of the ottoman. That would do for now. The first thing she did when she got her laptop out there was order a card table from Amazon on sale for $38.36.

THE FIRST THING THAT was ready for use in the new bathroom was the shower. Early, before the workers arrived, or later, when they were gone, Dani could relish a hot shower with decent water pressure from a head that wasn't dangling at a precarious angle. The tub, clean and white, made her happy.

A few days before they were going to start painting, Dani called Mike. He answered the phone like this: "Dani? Is that you? Are you okay?"

"Yes, I'm fine, Mr. Tarantino." Pause. "Mike. I'm calling with a question."

Mike waited for three seconds, but when nothing happened he said, "Okay, great, Dani. What's your question?"

"What color are they going to use? In the bathroom?"

Mike almost laughed but thought better of it. "I was going to head to Lowes and just see what's on sale."

"Lem has a book of paint colors," Dani offered.

"Okay, that's great. What are you saying?"

"I'd like to pick the color."

SHE CHOSE A VIBRANT apricot, and she wanted the trim to be white. She told Mike, "If you buy the paint, I'll paint the vanity myself." For that, she wanted a bright, cheerful green, like her favorite Castelvetrano olives.

The day the guys were painting the bathroom, Dylan spotted Dani out on the back stoop in cutoff shorts and a ratty baseball jersey, painting the drawers and sides of the vanity. The top and sink would be clean white, and the fixtures shiny nickel. She had asked Mike for a say in that too. Dylan peered through the biggest crack in the fence and said, "Hi, Dani. That looks great!"

Dani dropped her brush into the quart-sized can of green paint and could feel her heart accelerate. But, after retrieving the brush and wiping it, she turned to see—nothing. Then Dylan rounded the fence and headed to where Dani squatted. "Sorry I scared you."

Dani squinted, to see him better against the flat white glare of the autumn sky. She smiled and turned back to her work.

Dylan felt, if not invited, at least not rejected, so he moved closer and stood two feet away from her. They both looked at the vanity, watched the rhythmic brushstrokes, and in a minute Dylan said, "I love that color."

Dani dipped her brush. "Me too."

Rice Wine and Blowdarts

Bonnie J. Morris

IN 1993 I WORKED AS A PROFESSOR ON A SHIP. I JOINED 550 STUDENTS AND faculty on the global Semester at Sea voyage, which offers a college term of study aboard (then) the SS *Universe*, exploring twelve countries in a hundred days. I was one of the youngest professors on board and, in those pre-internet times, recorded all of my impressions in my journal. This story is a true account of my experience in Sarawak, on the island of Borneo, taking my students into the jungle as guests of a former headhunting tribe.

FOR SIX DAYS WE floated through the loveliest, smoothest waters I ever saw: the South China Sea. In those reflecting waters we saw ourselves. Each evening indescribable sunsets drew us all to gaze over the railings. The South China Sea was as smooth as glass, and as perfectly marbled. One could see the reflections of distant clouds in the water; the rose light and aqua water met in pillars of cloud. A world ringed in rose clouds and glass waves, a sea-lake of reflections, my brown bare feet up on the white railing, birds flying upwind and students murmuring, "I can't believe this is *ocean water*." Tankers passed by like slugs on the petal, carrying petroleum from the Persian Gulf. Dolphins played. At night many of us forsook our hot cabins to sleep on the top deck, underneath the exhilarating constellations.

For the faculty, particularly those of us who grew up during the 1960s, it was impossible to ignore our geographic position: we were somewhere off Hanoi, our starboard side facing Vietnam. These were the skies and waters seen by so many young Americans as they landed in a culture they'd never studied and prepared to kill the inhabitants. Watching our students, average age twenty or twenty-one, grapple with standards of community behavior aboard ship, reminded me that the average age of the American soldier in Vietnam was nineteen. Now I sailed, privileged as pie, past the countryside my nation helped devastate, past green land where the defoliants and Agent Orange toxins we spewed later emerged as cancers, deformities, children born without spines; and as a child myself in the late 1960s I marched, sang, and protested against this horror. My schooling, my choice of friends, my clothes, my adoption of a Vietnamese child through the Foster Parents Plan, all connected me to the struggle in Southeast Asia when I was young; but my own students on Semester at Sea lacked these memories. Thus I lectured on Vietnam all week. The "reward" would be a trip into Malaysia. And as we approached the port city of Penang, I finally had a moment to write in my journal:

If you could SEE the color of the water today—and a white bird circling, diving, circling, diving. I am watching flying fish and swimming birds, and I want again to PAY ATTENTION—to the big blue, the cloud life, the stories I'll bring back. Sunsets, like relationships, are often events one cannot photograph; smells, and tastes, like quick physical pains, are experiences one cannot bring home from Asia.

I was about to have the adventure of a lifetime, a trek into a longhouse to drink, eat, and dance with a tribal medicine man.

One of two Malaysian states—the other is Sabah—on the northern border of Borneo's island, Sarawak is home to the indigenous jungle peoples who, invaded by Western explorers earlier in history, earned racist publicity as "wild men" and cannibals. Assuredly, headhunting and the importance of the skull totem in tribal longhouse rituals have indeed been a critical part of Iban and Sea Dayak culture, although since World War II only the tattooed middle fingers of older men signify warrior experience. But the exaggeration of the greater

Borneo inhabitants' bloodthirstiness resulted in cruel exploitation and stereotyping.

As a child, one of my favorite picture books was Hilary Knight's *Where's Wallace?*, a hunt-and-find action story predating the derivative Where's Waldo? series by many years. Wallace, the orangutan (a species indigenous to Borneo) who perpetually escapes from the zoo to seek out urban adventure, hides out in an amusement park. When his keeper locates him, we are shown that Wallace cleverly disguised himself as the "Wild Man of Borneo" in the sideshow, or freak, area of the carnival. The readers—let us assume, children—are left to comprehend that these Wild Men so resemble apes that Wallace could pass as human—and that the display of actual humans from a distant culture is an acceptable form of modern, urban entertainment. Young readers end up feeling more sympathy for an animal's restriction in a zoo than for humans displayed as "freaks" in a carnival.

But the legacy of the caged man is real. *Ota Benga: The Pygmy in the Zoo*, by Phillips Verner Bradford and Harvey Blume, describes the exploits of Bradford's grandfather Samuel Phillips Verner, who captured tribal Africans for display at the Louisiana Purchase Exposition in 1903. Ota Benga, one of the men so displayed, was later caged at the Bronx Zoo and, yes, exhibited alongside an orangutan in the Primate House. This turn-of-the-century trade in human cargo, long after the Thirteenth Amendment abolished slavery, is very much a part of our American sideshow legacy. Eventually Ota Benga was released to the Howard Colored Orphan Asylum in Brooklyn; in the care of a minister, he converted to Christianity and eventually committed suicide.

To this day, carnival freak shows lure the curious to displays promising Wild Women or Primitive Women or actors dressed up as Wild Men of Borneo; I passed such a booth at a Maryland county fair on the very night before I left the US for my fall 1993 voyage on Semester at Sea. More troubling is the casual use of the racist metaphor in presumably feminist films: in *Fried Green Tomatoes*, young

Idgie plays in the woods while her mother scolds, "You look like the wild man of Borneo." This sort of remark might indeed have been overheard at the picnic of a Southern family of the 1920s, but why was it included in the film? It is nowhere in Fannie Flagg's book, *Fried Green Tomatoes at the Whistle Stop Cafe*, upon which the otherwise excellent movie is based.

I immersed myself in these issues because while most of our students planned to collapse on the beaches of Penang, I had volunteered to lead a party of twenty students and adult passengers to an Iban tribal guesthouse in the jungles of Sarawak.

THE JOURNEY TO SARAWAK's jungle had been a standard and very popular field trip option on Semester at Sea for years. Assisted by Sarawak's tourism bureau, I coordinated a three-day trek, which began as soon as we cleared customs in Penang. Our group of sojourners, armed with insect repellent, hiking boots, and hats, raced off to the airport for our flight into Kuching. In Malaysia, where the penalty for drug possession is death, and where much of the population is Muslim, strict demeanor and proper dress are a must for foreign visitors, and airport inspection was thorough. Our bug spray was confiscated, along with our puny Swiss Army knives. Changing planes in Kuala Lumpur, we temporarily sat in an airport where tropical birds flew in and out above our heads as a Dolly Parton video blared, subtitled "SEXY MUSIC. NOT FOR SALE."

Beautiful Malaysia was Jurassic Park–like with its ferns, green mountains, mists and flowers, palms, gigantic tree roots, and gnarled vines climbing mosaic stone fronts. Pepper, cocoa, rubber, and tapioca plantations fanned below us as we flew south toward the equator, eating the world's most interesting in-flight meal: fried banana, starfruit juice, bean-paste buns, and bamboo chicken with corn cake. As trip leader, I constantly had to count heads, answer questions, and deal with students' anxieties (the piano prodigy from Beverly Hills was sure he'd get malaria from a single mosquito bite, but all of us were taking heavy jolts of Lariam).

At Kuching, we met our guide for the trek, a soft-voiced and very pleasant young student named Joseph who was only too happy to share cultural information with a slightly older feminist professor. Kuching, the capital (and only) city of Sarawak where we slept that first night, is legendary for its gender-bending transvestite population, as David Duncan notes in his global bicycling adventure *Pedaling the Ends of the Earth*. My students, seduced by Sarawak's climate and beauty, raced around town beaming at local folk, casually inviting a group of Kuching women back to our hotel to discuss women's issues in Sarawak. It was only after two hours of spirited conversation that they realized these "female" informants were, in fact, male Kuching youths in drag. ("Will this count for my paper in women's studies?" wailed Laura.)

In Kuching the air was the temperature of one's body, like a movable bath. Scorpions scuttled across parking lots. The waterways were gently parted by painted taxi-ferries depositing women on either side of Kuching. But encroaching modernization and male privilege were also evident. Like an aggressive hornet, one young man buzzed his Jet Ski up and down the otherwise placid river; I learned he was the son of the city's highest official and owned the only Jet Ski in Sarawak.

Late at night I went into the hotel bookstore in a vain attempt to find books by or about the Iban women we were soon to visit. The only text was *Queen of the Headhunters*, about the wife of Sir James Brooke, the British explorer who had "discovered" the "natives." In the hotel bar my students were enjoying alcoholic drinks served in tropical headhunter-cartoon mugs. I thought about art imitating life, that our students' reference points for what they were about to see were only Indiana Jones films and Disneyland park rides: Pirates of the Caribbean, the Swiss Family Robinson Treehouse, Tom Sawyer Island.

In the morning we departed by bus and headed into the jungle, passing thatched and tin roofs, houses on stilts, fan trees, papaya and melon stands, upright pepper stalks, startled-looking palms, villages of sarong-clad schoolgirls. Joseph instructed us in the culture we would later encounter, explaining that in the Iban communities twenty-two families shared one longhouse, which typically did include a human skull in the rafters as a trophy of war. He described the tradition wherein the head-trophy (only male adult skulls were ever sought) was placed in a basket and soaked in river water for ten days, then brought into the longhouse for three ceremonies—during which women were not permitted on the veranda.

The bifurcation of roles in Iban culture meant only men were warriors. Traditionally, women demonstrated power through their art and economic skills, and this is still true today. Not only are women valued workers in pepper and rice harvesting, but their music, carving, and weaving today yield a source of income as well as practical or spiritual uses for the longhouse community. Hand tattoos are the mark of an exceptional woman weaver. Women also retain certain controls over courtship; in the ritual *ngayap*, a boy may visit a girl's bedroom but she may decline his visit. She may also sing *pantun*, a chant of flattery to the one she loves. There is emphasis on modesty, yet generosity and pleasure characterize male-female relations as well, we would soon see.

The most critical test we, as guests, would have to pass involved drinking ritually with the chief. Joseph warned us about the etiquette for drinking *tuak* (mild rice wine) and the more lethal *laagkau*. Custom mandated at least three toasts ("UHA!") and as many more as we could stomach before we correctly raised two fingers, Iban manners for begging off with thanks. The students, perpetually chafed by controls on their shipboard drinking, now burst into cheers at this unexpected requirement of jungle partying, and we drove on—mile after mile, hour after hour along one road toward the jungle of the Kasit River.

When at last our bus reached the riverbank, we found long dugout canoes (with hand-controlled outboard motors) waiting to take us to the Nanga Kasit guesthouse. We quickly divided into groups of four or five to a boat and disappeared into the jungle, our Iban pilots smiling back at us as the great adventure began.

OF ALL THE EXPERIENCES on the Semester at Sea voyage, this one stands out as the finest meeting between cultures, the blurriest border between hallucination and reality; a lifetime of camping out and, later, attending women's music festivals had prepared me for authentic simplicity and ritual among strangers. Upriver in a longboat I went with perfumed petals, blossoms, and vines falling out of the enormous tree canopies overhead and into my lap. In these trees live the world's largest butterflies and the "adultery birds," which daily check their mate's nest for seeds brought by a different suitor. Wild birds and crocodiles trailed the water, pigs and monitor lizards nuzzled the shore, solemn-eyed children watched from suspension bridges and longhouses and their own boats. We raced team against team during the hour-long journey, all of us screaming as our longboats powered up the shallow, narrow curves of river. Anything might live in that jungle: vipers, boars, monkeys, deadly spiders. In time we saw them all.

When we arrived at the guesthouse, perched high above the muddy bank, music and dance greeted us, and tattooed warriors clasped our hands. We walked up to the longhouse for the welcome ceremony, accompanied by bells—and at the entrance a wineskin was instantly plunged into my mouth, nipple-like. As instructed, I chugged down my first taste of satiny *tuak* and shrieked, "UHA!"

Our hosts were as affectionate and dignified as any large family welcoming guests. As trip leader from the ship, I won the place of honor next to the tribal medicine man, who placed a plaited grass crown on my head (much to my students' amusement). We observed that the longhouse was indeed long, cool, dim, with a few private rooms opening for the separate families' privacy, woven mats on the floor, and, yes, a skull in the rafters. Pigs, monkeys, roosters, and dogs ran in and out as we ate and drank and listened to drumming welcoming our arrival.

An adjacent longhouse with mosquito-netting over bed cubicles served as our group's quarters, and after the exciting welcome ceremony we repaired to this house to unpack and make supper. Joseph and several other men did all the cooking, with fresh ingredients from the roadside markets we'd passed earlier in the day: bits of chicken, ferns, bamboo, pineapple. I helped clean dishes afterward and befriended the women, who immediately asked (Joseph translated) if I was single, how many children I had. They each had five, they boasted. But few children over six were evident. Most were away at government schools, so that we enjoyed that particular company of the very old, the very young, and a few intermediary family members such as women artists still in childbearing years.

When we had washed from supper, we returned to the longhouse for three or four hours of terrific partying. Endless toasts preceded our formal introduction to the chief, a smiling man in an anachronistic Izod polo shirt. We had been forewarned that gifts must be presented, and each of us in turn offered our presents to the community—in most cases food items, particularly sweets and crackers, which along with the ritual drinking added to the ambiance of a clandestine riverside slumber party. The elders cheered and applauded each presentation of our gifts, and all items were immediately shared out equitably among the families in true collective dispensation. I gave a bracelet to the chief's wife, a strikingly handsome woman with a cast on her right arm—she'd recently fallen down a bamboo ladder. (This did not surprise us, as one bamboo deck rotted and broke under my feet the next day.)

After drinking the Iban equivalent of white lightning and properly honoring the chief by screaming aloud and hurling our emptied cups at his head, we watched dances by both men and women —choreographies both fierce and funny, solemn and seductive. As each dancer readied to perform, we offered sips from our cups of *tuak*, the sweet and flowery rice wine, and when each dancer finished, he or she went around our entire assembled circle and shook each hand. The continual touching broke down any remaining barriers not knocked flat by copious drinking, and soon we were dancing in an Iban conga line. My sarong kept falling off, much to the hilarity of the women present; as the revelry increased, we were treated to a masked drag dance, in which men performed with false breasts and simulated both pregnancy and breastfeeding. This pantomime-play on sex roles was a favorite with the Iban children. I noticed with interest that the baby doll used in this play was a blonde and Western toy.

Thunder, jungle bird calls, and crowing roosters, as well as bells and drums, made fine music as we grew sweatier and sweatier, guzzling wine and dancing in the arms of our hosts. Whatever sexual taboos existed relaxed considerably as I polkaed away with an elderly man and my male students bowed to Iban girls. I found myself accidentally crossing gender lines by drinking hard and asking women to dance. I linked feet with the Iban women for hopping games, my cup constantly refilled by men who roared approval. The liquor, fortunately, did not stupefy me, or create ill aftereffects the next day; it merely created a fountain of perspiration under my skin, and in the few photographs I permitted my students to take, I appear glistening wet.

Hours of singing and dancing later, the mood switched to business as our hosts set up a night market and invited us to barter for handcrafted wares. Here, too, affectionate rituals predominated, as each bargain was clinched by more handholding and smiling. Our dance partners were suddenly revealed as artists of incredible skill, displaying woven mats, knives, blow-darts, carved statues of humans and spirits, shell jewelry, model longboats, skull masks. I took care to buy one item from each family group; at the end of the night the chief put up a sheet painstakingly listing each family's distribution of sales and income.

To one young woman I gave a bracelet off my own hand. She in turn gave me a wooden one inscribed, "Remember Me Always."

* * *

THE FESTIVE COOPERATION THAT characterizes Sarawak's indigenous culture is a great contrast to the wrenching industrialization in mainland Malaysia—which has so uprooted and degraded women hired into multinational factory labor. The outside world has altered the Iban through missionaries, the separation of schoolchildren from home, the occasional Bart Simpson T-shirt on a toddler, and the destruction of rainforests for timber and land development. We knew that our visit served economic interests, that our gifts and purchases helped deflect poverty, and yet the ways of the Iban so unleashed our collective imagination that it was we who profited most from the shared time. In the longhouse, when I handed out American wildlife stickers as gifts, children and adults pasted them to their skins as personal adornment, a use I'd never considered. In the humidity the stamps easily clung to one's flesh. I found myself holding the hands of someone who wore my state bird, back home, pasted between his eyes.

There were students who reacted anxiously to being constantly patted, caressed, held, applauded, who were stunned to be in demonstrative company, whose own experiences had never included circle dancing and adult games of mischievous affection.

Television had replaced their grasp, their living contact. I, however, found peace in a living community of basic values: storytelling, dance, art, sharing, humor, generosity.

I BARELY SLEPT, DESPITE the comfortable guesthouse. Singing and animal sounds, strange creatures scampering over the thatched roof, kept me awake. In the morning we were instructed in manly arts—cockfighting and blowpipe lessons—which distressed some students; but as this too represented popular art forms I paid attention. Handed an enormous blowpipe about three or four feet long, I tried to hit the tree target, and on my second dart hit the bull's-eye—greatly impressing the male students in my group, none of whom could hit the mark. "You made it look easy," complained one, the ultimate compliment. The Iban men offered me a live piglet as a prize, but I had to decline, although I bartered for my own *sumpit* and *temilah* dart set.

We hated to leave. I grasped the warm hands of as many women as possible. "Aaahh!" they shouted, nodding at me: the he/she, the woman who played men's games, the woman who hit the mark, the childless warrior who took no husband. I shuddered to think of our hosts sold as sideshow displays, their presumed "wildness" luring missionaries and carnival barkers to capture and "civilize" them—into what? Workers trained in corporate industrial labor rather than cooperative living? Factory slaves whose art becomes a ceramic headhunter mug for the Holiday Inn bar?

On our return trek we walked through the jungle for some time before meeting the transport boats, noting rubber and tapioca trees, pineapple plants, the clay jars of graveyards, green vipers leering from low branches. Sweat soaked my T-shirt and pants. Finally we boarded longboats waiting in a cove, and took that last, refreshing, spray-flecked trip down the river, flowers literally falling into our hair from huge overhanging trees. I thought of the dance of the pods and blossom in Disney's *Fantasia*.

Driving back to the Kuching airport, we stopped at a rural cafe and ate stirfried ferns and peanut shrimp. By now we were accustomed to eating with our hands. But there was no time or modest space for me to change from my jungle-drenched clothes, so I, the "trip leader," who had taken care to wear a long dress and a spanking clean head scarf at the start of the journey into Malaysia, now stumbled into the Kuching airport covered in jungle droppings and peanut oil and feathers. I looked so disreputable and grimy that I was instantly stopped by police, separated from my group, patted down and frisked, and taken to a detention chamber; as I was being led away I overheard one student say to another, "Well, she's dead."

As I'd not seen a mirror in two days, I was mystified by all the fuss. It probably didn't help that I was wearing a blowpipe and poison darts strapped around my hips.

I stood nervously explaining to the officials that I had just escorted twenty students to an Iban longhouse. I explained that I loved Sarawak, loved Malaysia, was only carrying darts because they were a gift from our Iban hosts. Finally, one official glared at me. "So, you say you like Malaysia. Will you root for us in World Cup?"

Soccer, the universal language! With all my heart I gave thanks for those adolescent summers at Rainbow Soccer Camp in Chapel Hill, North Carolina. I assured my detainers that not only would I cheer Malaysia but that I was a soccer player myself. Somehow they interpreted this to mean that I had a starring role on some current professional women's team, and, hoping for a quick return to my students (who had all passed customs), I didn't bother to correct the illusion. Instead I demonstrated, on a handy grapefruit, a few fancy moves I'd learned at age fourteen, and the officials were so impressed I was finally let go. Once again, apparent "male" skill had raised my stature and served me well. There was no need to broadcast formally that in my athletic past I had, in fact, been the worst soccer player on the worst recreation league team in various small American towns.

When I walked through the barrier and into the women's restroom, I was delighted by my appearance. Limp petals, cobwebs, and leaves stuck to my shirt collar and crushed poisonous insects leaked from the soles of my boots. I was smeared with insect repellent and sunscreen, so sticky that road dust and agricultural fluff had nicely adhered to every inch. I reeked of rice wine, stirfried ferns, and rooster dung. As I admired my reflection I overheard a student reporting, "And then the airport police detained Professor Morris because she was so dirty she looked, you know, like the Wild Man of Borneo."

But our hosts had not been dirty, had not been wild.

Just like that, this student returned to the language of Western racism to make sense of what he'd seen.

Femininity and Pleasure: Observations on Wingfire

Jessica Burdg

Teach her that to love is not only to give but also to take. This is important because we give girls subtle cues about their lives—we teach girls that a large component of their ability to love is their ability to self-sacrifice. We do not teach this to boys. Teach her that to love she must give of herself emotionally but she must also expect to be given.

—Chimamanda Ngozi Adichie,
Dear Ijeawele, Or A Feminist Manifesto in Fifteen Suggestions,
Facebook, October 12, 2016

THE WOMAN TWIRLED IN FRONT OF THE TRIFOLD MIRROR OUTSIDE THE dressing rooms in the small vintage boutique—on display to the other customers in a way, but also blocked by a few racks of corduroy, suede, and velvet.

That's why I frequented this tiny shop in particular. So much well-worn texture, so much pre-loved, rich thread.

"I look best in warm colors. Reds, oranges," she said—to herself, in the mirror.

She had tried on one of the only items there that *wasn't* classified as vintage. In fact, the skirt was brand new—and hand-stitched by a local designer, who just happened to be in the store that day.

At the front of the boutique, the designer's dedicated rack stood. Many times, I had watched a shopper linger there, finger the soft material of the clothing, pausing. I'd done it myself, more than once. It was always as if we were both admiring the delicious fabrics and calling to mind other versions of ourselves, ones who might dare to wear something like what we momentarily held in our hands. When the thought would pass, the spell of the rack broken, we'd move on. In other words, these were "what if" clothes, and we all knew it. Lovely, but meant for someone else.

The skirts that hung there were statement pieces made of tulle and lace, light and fairy-like. They were primarily white and cream with differently hued underlays, ankle-length numbers with matching hand-stitched bandeau tops. Their flowiness was no doubt meant to entice bohemian-eyed passersby to wander inside, enchanted by the quirky femininity on display. Once inside, though, the what-if clothes proved too intimidating to try on.

But not, apparently, for everyone.

As the woman admired herself in the mirror, I admired her, quietly, from the gap between the end of the curtain and the end of my fitting room. She had to be in her fifties, her smooth, dark skin indeed well-suited for oranges, reds. Her two adult daughters groaned at how long it was taking her to make up her mind about the skirt. She did not, however, seem fazed. The fabric swirled around her, underneath a deep mauve with a white poof of an overlay. It looked to me like a wedding dress had been cut in half and then also somehow modpodged/ patchworked together to create something none of us had ever seen. The skirt was beautiful, in a word. The woman was beautiful, in a word. She looked like magic because I could tell she felt like magic.

"I never see *anyone* try these on," the designer said, her thrill audible. She strolled over to the woman in the mirror.

"Don't worry what the price says. We'll work it out."

The skirt-clad woman turned to her daughters, who looked back at her, nodding yes. The designer smiled. I smiled, and I wasn't even part of the interaction, technically. It no longer felt like a sale at that point. Instead, it was as if the shop and everyone in it was willing this magnificent woman in all her boldness, all her confidence, to take what was obviously hers. Nobody else would ever have that particular presence in that skirt, have that particular pleasure at twirling in front of the trifold mirror while wearing it. Nobody. No-body.

What essential elements of life that moment conveyed: for the skirt-maker, to create something beautiful and trust that someday, someone would appreciate it, would linger with it longer. To wait for the time someone would take her art and press it against something as sacred as a body. How essential, for the skirt-wearer, to feel so stunning. How rare an experience, to get to twirl in *anything* in front of not only the person who created it, but also the people who love you—all of whom are nodding, wanting you to have it, willing you to take it, catching a bit of secondhand joy at your simplest pleasure.

In "Like Light over This Plain" Rumi writes, "A moth flying into the flame says/With its wingfire, *Try this*."

The moth in the poem is flying to that which burns, that which licks the whole of darkness that surrounds it. It's simple, really: a living thing moving toward a heat source. Isn't that what we're all doing, in one way or another? How natural.

The woman in the mirror did what most shoppers would not do. She did what I still have yet to do, in that store. She used her wingfire. She tried. She knew her body and what she wanted to feel on it, and she let herself ask for and have it. All else be damned.

I am getting better about being as bold as the woman in the mirror (who *did*, by the way, get the skirt). In his song "Old Age," genre-crossing artist Masego sings, "Young girl, you don't know your body yet." On that same album, the smooth jazz saxophone sensually seeps in, catching you off guard. I kind of like that, being caught off guard. And I agree with Masego. There are so many ways to experience pleasure—from wearing something that makes you feel like a goddess to what goes on in heady darkness, and everything in between—and my openness to all those ways is much deeper now that I'm one of those old ladies. Now that I know my body and am letting her, more and more, ask for what she wants. Now that I know what I desire to touch and be touched by on the body of another. Now that I know that if the other body isn't there, my own can be enough, a willing companion.

I feel this most when lying between delicate sheets in an empty hotel room, which I like to do, feeling the cool fabric brush my bare skin, noticing each goosebump and how it got there, the space quiet. Looking back, in these moments, I have come the closest to knowing why the woman in the mirror was so taken with the skirt, because I've felt a little of that degree of affection for myself too. It's born of an admiration for our landscape of a body, the potential for pleasure always on our fingertips, always a flight-to-the-flame away, a love poem we keep inside, one we need only part our lips to whisper.

The Day I Flew

Mariah Julio

MY FRIEND ANNIE AND I STUFFED OURSELVES ON FOOD FROM THE LOCAL Chinese buffet.

"Annie, look at this," I said, laughing when I handed her the message from the fortune cookie.

"Travel and adventure feed your spirit," she read. "Perfect sentiment."

We are two retired women with AARP cards and itchy feet who are intent upon seeing as much of the world as possible until our bodies are too tired to move. Our trip to Alaska began the next day.

We chattered like chipmunks on the flight the next morning. Our first destination was Talkeetna, a town of about seven hundred people located at the base of Mt. Denali, the highest peak in North America. We had lodging at the iconic Talkeetna Roadhouse, which had served massive meals for those yearning to scale "the mountain" since the early 1900s.

Our excitement grew as we explored the town. Not because we planned to climb—we may be north of sixty, but we still have good sense. We planned to soar through the trees in the Denali Zipline Adventure, three hours and nine zips. Grannies gone wild.

No stranger to activity, I've spent years hiking, boating, and traveling to many destinations. Not to mention inline skating for a time.

This trip followed the death of my younger brother and a divorce that seemed to come out of nowhere. My future seemed eclipsed by confusion. With my confidence shredded, retirement wasn't shaping up anything like I imagined.

Annie set about helping me pull myself and life together. Born with a wider adventurous streak than I, ziplining was her idea. My initial underwhelming enthusiasm only fueled her determination to force me out of my shell of depression and help glue together pieces of my life.

After a splendid breakfast the next morning, Annie and I took our places on the first zipline platform. For a moment, I thought about a graceful exit when the staff couldn't find a helmet small enough to fit me. Worse luck, someone resurrected a child's helmet left in storage. A few minutes later, double harnessed and tethered to a thick steel cable above my head, I sincerely doubted my bold declaration of abundant common sense when I looked down at treetops.

I'm not usually afraid of heights. I've flown on planes many times and find liftoff exhilarating. This was not the same. No pretend security of an aircraft shell. No delusion of safety with a nearby oxygen mask and flotation seat. Thin air and a few lines separated me from wilderness below.

Captivated by the astounding vista of Alaska countryside and mountain range, I only required the gentlest push to fly across the first stretch of wire while the remainder of our party yelled encouragement from the deck behind me. The ground never looked lovelier covered with a carpet of white, star-shaped flowers. I learned from the guide later the blooms are dwarf dogwood, which flourishes in bitterly cold climates. In Indiana, dogwood is a small, flowering tree covered with white or pink blossoms. This excursion combined my love of natural beauty with the element of surprise that abounds in Alaska. Cool wind on my face felt exhilarating when I landed at the next stand of trees.

True to its brochure, the Denali Zipline Adventure provides a variety of activities designed to appeal to diverse appetites.

"Get ready to rappel," our guide announced.

"What is repel?" I blurted.

The guide smiled and coached the first pioneer. Turns out,

rappel requires sliding through airspace with the aid of a rope and sheer grit. I couldn't spell it let alone have the courage to do it. I quietly stepped to the end of the line.

While all the members of our group stared up at me after taking their turns, I relaxed at the instructor's command, took a deep breath, and sailed out into the atmosphere on a rope and a prayer. My feet connected with the ledge below. Despite a pounding heart, my focus steadied while I prepared for the remainder of the journey.

On our final and longest zip, we careened six hundred feet across the Reflection Pond rimmed with spruce trees right out of a Bob Ross painting. I landed tired, hungry, and invigorated by wings I didn't know I had.

At the end of our journey, I pulled my camera out and began taking another round of photographs. Pictures I took at the beginning of our excursion show an eclectic group of people, including a couple honeymooning and another celebrating a milestone anniversary, eager and delighted to begin new chapters in their lives. The same group at the end of our tour looked a smidge bedraggled but heartened by the freedom we experienced encased in leather straps and hanging from a wire.

On the zipline trip, I conquered my fears of walking on suspension bridges, dangling in midair, and crashing into deep water.

Retirement will never be what I dreamed during years of marriage, working, and volunteering. Stretching my imagination to include new experiences adds another facet to a time I've long anticipated. A golden season to explore new beginnings and pursue unfulfilled dreams tabled somewhere along the way.

The zipline experience helped me understand that I am chained only by my concept of myself. Life is filled with unexpected challenges. I'm focused on seeing the blue behind the storm clouds.

I'll never meet the author of the fortune cookie prediction. The timely views spurred my trip into the unknown and fostered a desire for more exploration of our beautiful world. That spectacular day in Alaska, I took flight in new and wonderful ways.

on the day i shaved my head

Kaitlyn Zeran

on the day i shaved my head i cried 3 times on the day i shaved my head i wore a men's t-shirt and purple leggings is this what it means to be a woman? on the day i shaved my head i googled the definition of feminine i swear i have wanted to do this my whole life i swear i want to let go on the day i shaved my head i told four people my plans three of them told me not to do it why? i cried at their responses on the day i shaved my head it was sunny and bright and i felt the same way inside on the day i shaved my head we started at the base of my neck and moved up i cried from laughter half way through on the day i shaved my head i wrote down all the reasons why i wanted to: freedom, to put my energy towards better things, what does it mean to be beautiful? on the day i shaved my head i realized the wild woman inside me on the day i shaved my head a new beginning i talked on the phone with an old friend and she told me she was proud on the day i shaved my head i smiled and laughed every time i saw my reflection on the day i shaved my head i danced around my friends singing to the music on the day i shaved my head i questioned everything "to be yourself in a world that is constantly trying to make you something else is the greatest accomplishment" on the day i shaved my head for the first time in my life i thought about what i truly wanted and felt instead of what society wanted and felt on the day i shaved my head when i looked at myself i cried endlessly tears of joy free wild growth love let go

Genesis

Yael Shoshana Hacohen

IN JUNE, THE DESERT BECAME EVEN MORE OF A DESERT. THE DUST SETTLED ON everything, between my toes, in my socks, in my cotton underwear, in my ponytail. Like how my mother used to tuck me into bed, the training base was blanketed under a thick layer of heat and sand.

The commander's course was a no-bullshit environment. I shared a small room with five women. The army dispersed one of us to each squad. Since we were the first women integrated into Bahad 1, the commander training base, we were offered the best room on the floor. My cot was cool in the morning and warm at night. And don't even get me started on the showers. Every soldier I know can always remember a base by its showers, and the showers at Bahad 1 were exceptional. Each stall had a blunt copper pipe with no showerhead and a single lever to turn the water on and off. There was no way to control the temperature; the pipe always gushed hot water. It may not sound like much, but let me tell you, after a long day of training, there was nothing like it. Since each squad had different training schedules, the girls' shower was always unoccupied. Each one for herself, you could say.

Israelis have a special word that makes a woman feel like a girl, *hamuda*, which translates roughly to sweetheart. It was my commanding officer's usual nickname for any woman he saw around the base, including our forty-three-year-old lieutenant colonel, even though he gritted that one out between his teeth.

My CO was the kind of self-proclaimed feminist who would always single me out. During Krav Maga training he explained to the group, "Always pick off the easiest target first," then he would point at me. He polished it off by adding, "You're up, *hamuda*." Taking that step forward was the longest step I ever had to take. The whole squad staring, nodding their head in perfect anticipation. What exactly did they want? What did they expect? I stood there, maybe twenty inches away from my CO, while he went on and on. He was going to show the most effective way to body slam a person, which involved the element of surprise. Then he whipped around, grabbed the lapels of my uniform, and brought me so close I could smell his shampoo. He kicked my right shin and simultaneously knocked my shoulder to the ground.

They tell me the fight or flight response takes only three seconds to initiate. The time it takes to pucker your lips, to focus a camera. The time it takes an African horned lizard to eat forty-five ants one at a time. I did not fight; instead I dusted myself off and returned to my spot in line, my shin sore, my hair out of place. The whole squad looked at me with two parts pity, one part superiority. *Hamuda* became my nickname throughout the base.

From there, everything changed. Little things really: the squad stopped looking me in the eye. They set their alarm clocks for fifteen minutes before I woke up. They had their inside jokes, their coy smiles, exchanged without words. They shared their laundry suds, their candied orange peels. As if I did not own the secret password or did not understand the rules of the game. They went out together on weekends, got drunk, and could not stop laughing.

One Tuesday, my commanding officer was going to demonstrate how to pull the weakling out of the army line, and he walked straight up to me and yanked my shield forward. I looked my commander right in the eyes, then I punched him in the face. He fell like a peacoat falling off its hook. Without a single word, I returned to my place in the line.

It changed nothing, or almost nothing. I was still known as *hamuda*, the squad still huddled together, the way men are sometimes taught to do. I didn't win any accord, award, or distinction during the entire course. No one even said a word to me about that one contained act. There was no moral to this story really, except only to say that if you ask me what adrenaline tastes like, it tastes like candied orange peels; I knew it almost immediately when I tasted it in my mouth.

Every Witch a Woman

Natasha Ayaz

IT WAS A DAY THAT TOUCHED PALMS WITH YESTERDAY AT EVERY PERIMETER.
The overnight rain had left the earth in slickness ripe for sinking, soft
and slurping enough that lost earrings, vials of teenage tears,
Tupperware lids, and entire eras past could all be just barely sensed
below the surface. The clouds, clogging the sky with slate, could have
concealed lurking swordsmen, cold corpses, the murder weapon. Even
the dog, mangy though he was, could smell something sour in the air
that made him growl low and cling closely to Matilda, who had chosen
a bad day to run away from home. The forest started behind her
father's house and ended nowhere in sight, which was exactly where
she wanted to be. She slid through the mud in her red rain boots,
fingering a switchblade in her pocket like a secret. The contents of
Matilda's satchel were as follows: a jar of jellybeans, ten dollars, two
dog treats, a *Farmers' Almanac* from thirty years ago, and a photograph
of her mother.

Before her mother's heart suddenly stopped, before her father
began dating a stream of Botox barbies, and before she began plotting
her escape into the woods, Matilda would fall asleep to her mother
telling her the story of the old woman in the trees. The old woman
lived in a house made of live branches that bent to her will. To
illustrate this detail, Matilda's mother would shake her long arms so
that her gold bracelets clanged together. Once, two children
disappeared forever into the woods and it was widely reported that

they had been cooked alive and consumed by a witch. Their father and stepmother were, ostensibly, beside themselves with grief, but what no one ever knew was that the children had run away from home. They hated the stepmother, who ate only romaine lettuce and ripped the sleeves off their mother's dresses, and so they ventured into the world on their own. When they came across the old woman in the trees, she offered to raise them there in her natural oasis, and they accepted with glee. Sometimes, Matilda's mother said with her eyes fixed on the bedroom window, you can still see them playing tag among the leaves if you look closely enough.

Matilda watched the sky above her kaleidoscope into foliage and cirrostratus cloud while she plunged deeper into the woods. The dog stayed vigilantly by her side, enduring the cold muck on his paws for his loyalty. It took approximately twenty minutes of walking for Matilda to break out the jellybean reserves. For a moment, holding the rainbow capsules in her palm, she considered dropping a trail of them behind her like the kids in the story, but that was silly and she didn't plan on going back home, anyway. She ate them as she continued on her way, giving every third bean to the dog, who swallowed them whole. There was no sign of any tree-dwelling children, and the forest was silent, as though the rain had flushed out life. There was no path. They marched forward on good faith alone. After half the jellybean supply was depleted, the dog began to snarl. Matilda turned in the direction of his malice to see a tall man standing alone between two firs. He wore a flannel jacket and baseball cap, his face was obscured by a parched gray beard, and he carried a rifle as long as tomorrow.

There was another tale her mother used to tell, when the moon was slanted across the sky and Matilda asked for one more story before bed, about a sleeping princess. She lay on a bed of silk for a hundred years, until brambles and vines circled her ankles and dragon lilies bloomed through the cracks in the bedroom walls, until she lay on a bed of moss and mice. At this point in the story, Matilda's mother would snake her long, cool fingers around her daughter's ankles, tickling the soles of her feet until she screamed. The princess's parents, the royals, made a performance of publicly mourning their daughter day in and day out. They would stand on their bejeweled balcony and weep onto the crowds below. Somehow, they stayed alive the entirety of the hundred-year slumber (so eat your spinach, Matilda, her mother said with mock austerity). The royals blamed the somnolence on the fairy godmother, who had swooped in and cursed the child when she was born. What the public didn't know, or the queen for that matter, was that the king had blackmailed the fairy godmother into casting the sleeping spell. You see, he always wanted a son instead, with whom he could play polo and guzzle ale and feel up the skirts of ladies-in-waiting. And that, Matilda's mother would say, is why you should always keep your eyes wide open.

The man swung the rifle over his shoulder and walked toward Matilda and the dog. She would have tried to run but her feet had gone leaden in her boots. When the man reached them, he took off his cap and squatted down to her level, smiling through his unwashed scruff.

"Now, what are you doing out here alone?"

The dog stepped in front of Matilda and barked dictatorially.

"We're just walking," Matilda said, taking a step backward.

"What's in the knapsack, then?" The man nodded toward her bag, scratching his silver sideburns.

"Toys," Matilda said, like a question.

"You know what I think?"

Matilda shook her head. The man gave the woods a circular glance.

"I think you're having a little run away from home on this fine Sunday morning. Lucky a nice man like me found you." Matilda shook her head again, feeling for the switchblade in her pocket and telepathically summoning the dog to bite the man in the nose. He did not receive the message. A high wind howled through the trees like a woman in labor.

"Look what I have," the man said, pulling a lollipop out of his pocket. "You look like you could use a snack."

"No, thank you."

"Come on, take it," he said, the smile peeling off his face like a sticker. "Pretty little girl like you deserves all the candy in the world." Matilda turned to run deeper into the woods, but he grabbed her arm with a gloved hand and dug his fingers into her skin.

"That hurts," she choked out, wishing she had never left her father's house, wishing her mother was alive, wishing the dog would turn three-headed and bite off a piece of the man in every mouth. The dog, doing his best, lunged for the man's calf only to be kicked aside.

"Hey," a voice rang through the woods, "let go of my daughter."

The man released Matilda's arm as a woman came running through the trees toward them.

"What do you think you're doing?" the woman yelled at the man, taking Matilda by the shoulders and moving her behind her back.

The man stared her down like a deer through a rifle scope before responding. "The girl was lost. I was helping her find her way home. Shouldn't let your kid out in the woods alone," he grumbled, walking away with his hands in the air.

"You're lucky I'm not pressing charges," the woman called after him.

When the man disappeared into the trees, she knelt before Matilda and cupped the girl's face in her shaking hands.

"Now, don't be scared, sweetie. It's going to be okay. Are you hurt?"

Matilda shook her head. She had never seen this woman before in her life.

When Matilda turned eight, her mother brought a bowl of chocolate cherries into bed for them to eat while she told her the story of the sorceress on the island. She was a beautiful woman, the sorceress, with a maze of curls and a mouth like a peeled plum. Matilda's mother, however, had whip-straight hair and lanceolate eyes, and Matilda always chose to imagine the sorceress that way instead. The island was her domain, and she kept it bustling with flora and fauna in complete harmony, until the day that a ship of men docked at her shore. She watched from her tower as they strode across the beach, hacked through her forest, and approached the gates of her home. They broke the latch with their pistols and stormed her halls, slashing paintings and slaughtering her pets, until finally they entered her chambers, where she stood waiting. Upon witnessing her glow, they began fighting over who would be the first to take her, creating an order for their violation. Riding on the power of her fury and righteousness, the sorceress rose like a star until she touched the high ceiling. If you insist on behaving like monsters, she bellowed, your outside shall match your inside. Then, with the rotation of a single finger, she transformed them into formless, sexless urchins with a life span of one day. You know, most stories say she turned them into pigs, Matilda's mother clarified, but that isn't true. They deserved much worse.

The strange woman wore hiking boots with Sharpie flowers and a bandanna around her dense curls. When Matilda told her the address of her father's house, she started leading the way confidently to the west, holding Matilda's hand all the while. The dog trotted alongside them, wagging his tail at the woman's presence.

"I could see that man talking to you from my house," the woman said. "I see him shooting in the woods sometimes, killing innocent animals. I always knew he was trouble."

"Your house?" Matilda asked, looking around.

"You can just barely see the roof through the trees over there," the woman said, pointing. "I live in the woods so I have privacy for my painting."

Matilda squinted to make out the wooden cabin. She almost didn't want to ask, being nine years old now and on the cusp of doubt, but she did anyway.

"Are you a witch?"

The woman laughed, then abruptly stopped when she saw Matilda's expression. "I'm an artist, but let me tell you a secret," she said before putting a palm around her mouth covertly, "all women are witches."

The forest started to thin around them, the sky claiming more space between the branches.

"In school, we learned about how people threw witches in the water to see if they would float."

The woman looked down at Matilda. "And what do you think about that?"

"I hope most of them pretended they didn't know how to swim," Matilda said.

They walked in silence for a moment. The woman looked like she had been called upon to save a life with words and was finding the right ones.

"You know, Matilda," she said, stopping to look the girl in the eyes, "a lot of people think the trick is to not let the men know you can swim, but that's not it. The trick is to become the water. The trick is to pull them in and drown them deep inside you. You drown them deep inside you and then you spit them onto shore."

Rewilding

Tracy Rose Stamper

Once I remembered that I had the wholeness
of the horizon to breathe into, I left the
whole
damn
building
behind.
While I knew it to be true that *"when one door closes, another opens,"*
that only mattered if I stayed inside. Four walls could no longer
  contain me.

Trees marking the edge of wild welcomed me. Hungry. Scraggly
  barked boughs
stripped me bare of pinstripes—the faux snake's shed skin of constriction.
Sumptuous, shiny new. Electric.
Slipping into the crevices, I took teatime with the trees.
Stinging nettle tincture and tea sweetened by bees' honey.
Stepping into the wild air, I stargazed infinity.
Dandelions danced as, together, we swirled stardust.
Lavender tendrils tended to my heart. Traces of phoenixes feathered
  my nest.
I came to rest in moonbeams spinning a cocoon of silks. Tenderized by
  tears.
Waterfalls washed away remnants of yesterday.

Savoring the seasons' lessons, I rooted to rise, pushed petals to the skies,
dropped dead leaves, grieved. Grieved. Grieved.
I studied the lioness. Snails. Watched wild dogs' tails.
I learned to love. And sting. Me. My own fierce wild thing.
Wandering through wildflowers and wonder, I braided my hair with
   clover and dreams.
I was swimming slipstreams when canyons called. Oceans coaxed.
I escaped into the seascape, met mountains, barefooted over forest floors.
Walking woods, I—once again—became my own wild moonchild.

Beckoning blossoms frolicked and sipped sunbeams with me.
We drank daylight down. Come night, moonshine quenched.
Mother Moon got me punch drunk on peonies' poetry. Consensually.
Roots dug down into earth, fingers finding their way
into intuitively traced mud paint. Warrior woman.
Stripes of Water with Earth announced celebrated clavicles,
hugged heralded hips, drew down to ground breastbone.
Raging tender heart anchored, flaming full of dusk's urgency.

Unmovable as a mountain standing tall, spine aligned with star wishes,
I now perch in my coral throne. Starfish radial symmetry.
Untamed. Unnamed. Unapologetic.
Rocked by the rhythm of the sea, you can hear me sing
of how it took waves of brave to refind me, rewild myself free,
and unbecome so as to simply be.
Freedom taught me to live beyond their doors.

I am the rainbow's end. Listen.
You'll hear me in the call of the loon.
If you dare, you, too, can find yourself there.

Contributors

MELINA VANCHIERI lives just outside Washington, DC, with her cat, her fern collection, and probably too many rocks. She was published twice as a teenager and is very excited to be published again as an adult.

SUE STAATS lives and writes in Sacramento, CA. Her story "That Kiss" is part of the collection *Hardpan*, twelve short stories bound together by the theme of personal reinvention, or rediscovery. Her fiction and poetry have been published in the *Los Angeles Review*, *Graze Magazine*, *Farallon Review*, *Tule Review*, *Late Peaches: Poems by Sacramento Poets*, *Sacramento Voices*, and others. She earned an MFA from Pacific University and was runner-up for the Gulf Coast Prize in Fiction and a finalist for the Nisqually Prize in Fiction. Her stories have been performed at both the Sacramento and Davis reading series Stories on Stage, and she has read her work at the SF Bay–area reading series Why There Are Words and Babylon Salon. For six years, she served as the director and curator for Stories on Stage Sacramento, and Sue continues to contribute interviews and other web content for the reading series.

PATRICIA SCHULTHEIS grew up in Bridgeport, CT, in a Polish-American family. Struck by polio when she was six years old, she became an introspective, moody child, who found great solace in reading. After graduating from Catholic schools and Albertus Magnus College in New Haven, she moved to Baltimore in 1965, where she taught school, got married, began a family, and had a career in public relations. During those early years in Baltimore, she observed that the city's civic code of decorum was more deeply inscribed than Bridgeport's, more informed by history, and more poisonous when violated. After having several dozen freelance articles and essays published while working full time, Patricia turned to writing fiction in her mid-fifties, and her observation about Baltimore's cultural mores became the foundation for her award-winning short story collection, *St. Bart's Way* (Washington Writers' Publishing House, 2015). She is also the author of *Baltimore's Lexington Market* (Arcadia Publishing, 2007) and *A Balanced Life*, a memoir (All Things That Matter Press, 2018). She now divides her energy between fiction, lyrical nonfiction, and book reviews. Several dozen of her short stories and essays have been published in national and international literary journals. Her work has been included in anthologies that also include stories by such distinguished authors as Alice McDermott and Annie Proulx. She has served on the editorial boards of the *Baltimore Review* and *Narrative* and twice has been awarded fellowships by the Virginia Center for the Creative Arts. She has won additional awards from the *Litchfield Review*, Winning Writers, the League of American Pen Women, Memoirs Ink, and the Fitzgerald Writers' Conference. She also has taught in the Odyssey Program of Johns Hopkins University, from where she earned master's degrees in 1973 and 2006. A widow, she continues to live in Baltimore, a city whose slow adaptation to change and sometimes quirky outlook mirror her own. She has two grown sons and five grandsons.

JESSICA MCDOUGALD is a thirty-year-old wife, mom, graduate student, and clergy woman living in Raleigh, NC. Poetry is her heart's native tongue.

ALYEA PIERCE, Ed.M is an award-winning author, educator, and international speaker and performance poet. As a black woman writer, her mission is to focus on what stories are not being told, and as a first-generation Caribbean-American, she strives to always be conscious of what experiences make us who we are. Always aiming to listen to the voices of the unheard, Alyea centers her creative projects around the exploration of Latino and Caribbean histories, the celebration of all things woman, and the untold narratives of marginalized persons to examine identity development of youths through creative writing. She is a Fulbright and National Geographic Storytelling Fellow in Trinidad and Tobago who has performed her spoken word poetry at countless TEDx events, and is published, both online and in print, including in *The Guardian*, the *New York Daily News*, *The Caribbean Writer*, *Autism Speaks*, and *Rutgers Today*.

LEEANNE R. HAY is a freelance writer in North Texas. She has been published in the *Dallas Morning News*, *DFW Child* magazine, and many other regional print and online publications. In 2016, her story "The Children Left Behind" about the children of opioid drug users was awarded the Ten Spurs Prize at the Mayborn Nonfiction Literary Conference national competition. "Climbing the (White) Ladder to Success" is her first published fiction. Find her online at www.LeeanneRebicHay.weebly.com or @LeeanneRH.

ANIL CLASSEN was born in 1977 and spent his first twenty-one years in the seaside city of Port Elizabeth, South Africa. He is a German writer of Indian descent living in Switzerland, with an academic background in psychology, English, and journalism. He divides his time between Zurich, Hamburg, and Cape Town, each of these being called home at one stage of his life. In his free time, he enjoys travel, which provides him with plenty of material for hobbies including blogging and photography, as well as inspiration for his writing and cooking. His current work, which deals with the journey of an Indian family documented through their love affair with food, has been shortlisted for the 2020 Spotlight First Novel Award. "Hercules" is his first published short story.

THEA SWANSON holds an MFA in writing from Pacific University in Oregon. She is the founding editor of *Club Plum Literary Journal*, and her flash fiction collection, *Mars*, was published by Ravenna Press in 2017. Thea's work can be found in many journals. Find her writing at theaswanson.com.

In June of 2014, VLADA TEPER spent five-plus hours daily dancing with US dancers and a professional Cuban dance troupe, in Santiago de Cuba. It was intense, highly challenging, sensual, and exhilarating to be let into the secrets of myriad Cuban dance forms by celebrated professionals and beautiful humans. Her poem "In Love" is a snapshot. Vlada's essays and fiction have been featured in *Perspectives* on KQED and the MishMash Writer's Salon. Her poetry has appeared in the *Potomac Journal* and *The Mind's Eye*. An alum of the Squaw Valley Writers Workshop, Vlada teaches high school, and is a recipient of the 826 Valencia Teacher of the Month Award. Vlada is the founder of I M U, Inspiring Multicultural Understanding, intercultural and social justice leadership programs for teens. And yes, she is an avid, wild dancer.

PAMELA O'HARA is a longtime tech entrepreneur and proud Providence Geek. She has cofounded a number of tech businesses, civically minded nonprofit organizations, and political projects. She currently serves as an advisor to the Social Enterprise Greenhouse and Rhode Island Food Bank. She earned a BA in English from the University of Richmond and enjoys creative writing, sailing, and cooking for her three dietarily diverse teenagers who occasionally appreciate it.

LISA FRANSSON took seed in a forest in southern Sweden where she was brought up on a diet of dark fairy tales and Norse mythology. As a teen she washed up on the shores of southern England where she now writes and breathes by the sea. Her short fiction has been published in *The Dark Mountain Project*, *The Dawntreader*, *The Forgotten and The Fantastical 4*, and *The Best of British Fantasy*. She also has two children's picture books to her name that she wrote in her native Swedish: *Älgpappan* and *Beckmörkret*. More information and contact details can be found at www.lisafransson.com.

SABRINA STRAND is an educator in Silicon Valley, CA, where she leads her department and shares her love of poetry with junior high and high school students. Her most memorable poetry experience was in Bali, Indonesia, where she ran several workshops for adults through the program Unsettled. She has also served as a judge for Poetry Out Loud, an annual competition sponsored by the National Endowment for the Arts. Besides poetry, Sabrina's other great love is performance, and she has been involved in many choirs and community theater productions over the years. She is a strong believer in the power of stories to shape and heal the world both around us and within us. Follow her on Instagram at sabrinastrandpoetry.

JACQUELINE M. GRYPHON of Portland, ME, describes writing as her "avocation, vocation, and employment for most of my life." She has been a copywriter, journalist, playwright, and poet. She has been published in anthologies, received awards for her poetry, and is an award-winning playwright whose work has been produced on stage. Currently, she is working on a new collection of poems, *Calling over Water*, that is slated for publication in 2021. She belongs to the Maine Poets Society and the Audubon Society of Pomfret, CT, where she'll be writer-in-residence this summer on the Audubon's 168-acre Trail Wood nature preserve, a week-long opportunity to experience nature while writing and editing her book. A native of Connecticut, Jacqueline recently moved to Maine and is active in several arts and organizations.

VANESSA PARK has written and edited professionally most of her life, currently with her own business, Vanessa's Red Pen. She taught writing for many years and also works in marketing and development for nonprofits. Vanessa studied writing at the University of Virginia and also has an MFA from Columbia University. Her work has previously been published in the *New Delta Review*. Originally from NYC, she currently lives on the island of Nantucket, thirty miles off the coast of Massachusetts, with her cat Boo Radley.

BONNIE J. MORRIS is a women's studies professor and historian, now a lecturer at the University of California at Berkeley, where she teaches the popular course Sports and Gender in US History. An archivist and scholar of American feminism, she is the author of sixteen books, including *Women's History for Beginners* and *The Feminist Revolution*, which was selected by *Oprah Magazine* as a must-read for women's history month. She is a historical consultant to the Smithsonian Institute, the AP US history exam, Disney Animation, the State Department's International Visitor Leadershp Program, the Global Women's Institute, and Pacifica Radio Archives. From 1994 to 2017, she taught women's history for the women's studies programs of both Georgetown and George Washington University in Washington, DC, where she first developed the women's sports course that attracted so many student athletes. Over a twenty-five-year period, her classes enrolled Olympic athletes, one of the Los Angeles Dodgers, and a crown prince; she also taught for the global Semester at Sea program, American University, and St. Mary's College, and became a consultant for Harvard University's athletics program. Her interviews on the growth of women's sports today may be found on C-SPAN and in publications around the world. Learn more at www.bonniejmorris.com.

JESSICA BURDG is a writer with a passion for personal narratives, creative nonfiction, and poetry. A journalist by trade, she uses her desire to learn about people and bring their stories into the world as a ghostwriter and manuscript creative at Scribe Media. Jessica has made a career helping authors turn their ideas into books; her first, *More Than a Diagnosis*, will be published this year. Jessica's essays and articles have been featured in multiple magazines and anthologies. Her essay on mental health was a finalist for the 2019 Conger J. Beasley Jr. Award for Nonfiction. After decades of only being lovingly displayed behind a refrigerator magnet in her late grandfather's kitchen, her poetry is now found at *Entropy Magazine*—and she knows he would be proud. Jessica is a mother, experience-enthusiast, and music lover. She enjoys traveling, running, and underlining meaningful finds in her growing collection of hard-copy books and newspapers. She lives in the Midwest with her young daughters, who mean everything. Jessica cares about social and economic equality, children's literacy, women's rights, and the differently abled community. She is active in the nonprofit space and is the founder of Project Penpal (www.projectpenpal.org), a foundation that fosters connection among lonely seniors in assisted living facilities with volunteer penpals around the country. She is the editorial chair of Who Is Carter and The Brain Possible, two organizations that work tirelessly to support the differently abled community and those with pediatric brain injuries. Jessica also volunteers with Lead to Read, a project that pairs adult mentors/readers with elementary-aged children in under-resourced school districts in her area. As are all human beings, Jessica is a work in progress. She also always has several works in progress; you can see what they are at www.JessicaBurdg.com.

KAITLYN ZERAN is a recent graduate from Western Washington University where she received her BA in English with an emphasis in creative writing. She resides in the ever beautiful Bellingham, WA. Nestled quietly in the upper PNW, she enjoys reading, painting, and writing in experimental forms. This is her first publication.

YAEL HACOHEN is a PhD student at UC Berkeley. She has an MFA in poetry from New York University, where she was an NYU Veterans Workshop fellow, international editor at *Washington Square Literary Review*, and editor in chief at *Nine Lines Literary Review*. Her poetry and short stories appear in *Prairie Schooner*, *Poetry Review*, *Bellevue Literary Review*, *Every Day Poets* magazine, *Nine Lines*, and many more. She was a finalist in the 2015 Glimmer Train Very Short Story Competition, the 2015 Consequence Prize in Poetry, and the 2013 MSLexia Poetry Prize for Women.

NATASHA AYAZ is a fiction writer and graduate of Bard College, where she studied written arts and literature. After completing her undergraduate studies, she moved back home to Boston where she is currently working on a collection of short stories. Her writing has previously appeared in *The Louisville Review* and is forthcoming in *Narrative Magazine*.

TRACY ROSE STAMPER dances with words. Her middle name is the most significant word she has written lately during these days asking us to rise. She lives in St. Louis with two beloved humans, two rescue beagles, and two whimsical wind sculptures. She is a columnist at Rebelle Society, contributing author of Anna Linder's *The Book of Emotions*, and has had work appear (or soon to appear) in *Dime Show Review*, *Drunk Monkeys*, *Feels*, and *borrowed solace*. You can find her at https://www.facebook.com/DancingPenTracyStamper.

Made in the USA
Monee, IL
04 March 2021